Funny's The Word

Alton Douglas

Published by Saron Publishing in 2023

ISBN-13: 978-1-913297-44-2
Also available as an ebook
978-1-913297-45-9

Saron Publishers
Pwllmeyrick House
Mamhilad
Mon
NP4 8RG

saronpublishers.co.uk
info@saronpublishers.co.uk
Follow us on Facebook and Twitter

Funny's The Word

Alton Douglas

For more of Alton's books,
visit
altondouglas.co.uk

ACKNOWLEDGEMENTS

Once again, I would like to thank the collection of reprobates who make my life what it is:

Pete Lindup: An excellent musician, comic and cartoonist, who seems to have more friends than you can shake a stick at - and that's his idea of a good time.

Terry Reeves: Any problems we have with our computer and Terry has the answer. He is also personally responsible for the necessary annual truck-load of coffee beans delivered to our house.

Our friend, Ken Windsor: He is always there when we ring him with queries. Completely ignoring our calls.

My nephew, Keith Price: Or, as I christened him, 'General Factotum'. (Fortunately, he doesn't own a dictionary.)

Jo: My long-suffering wife or, as someone once called her, 'A tomato to the cause.'

In all seriousness, I must pay tribute to the late Rowland Lindup (Pete's dad) for the wonderful cover cartoon depicting my time as a television warm-up comic.

Any errors in this book are certainly not of my making. I was out that day.

Back to the days of the Working Men's Clubs when the Entertainment Secretaries would write about the acts and club activities. Here are a few notes they made at the time - and if not, they should have:

The turn last Saturday was 'Michael, the Boy Soprano'. I think we booked him just in time for his second childhood.

I must apologise on behalf of the committee but we forgot Remembrance Sunday.

I was sorry to hear that the popular accordionist Brenda Moult has had to retire after her recent bust enlargement.

We had to ask the Mormon Choir to sing some quieter hymns when the heavy metal group, in the next room, complained about the noise.

It was a shame about the accident when Charlie Davenport was invited to participate in the knife throwing act. Someone should have told him that the artiste did the throwing.

When we booked the singer, the agent said that he would be singing his recent hit. I thought that he would have known some other songs as well.

I don't know whose idea it was to book a fire eater for Burns Night.

Melody Sings has always been very popular in our club so I was pleased to book her when I heard she had a new-look act. Personally, I don't think that the beard is a good idea.

When their bill matter said, 'An hour of solid laughter', I thought that meant the audience.

Following the costume competition, there were several complaints about the horrific costume worn by the Chairman's wife. Unfortunately, she was not a participant.

Next week, our act will be 'Ernesto and his Performing Cats'. The gimmick is that they don't do what he wants them to do, they do what they want to do.

I can't see any point in booking the Spencer Twins. When you have seen one of the girls, you've seen both of them.

The agent assured me that the escapologist was bound to be a success.

I said to the ventriloquist, 'What a funny way to earn a living. You might just as well talk to yourself.'

I must admit that I had slight misgivings when the Frank Sinatra Tribute Act opened with *You ain't nothin' but a hound dog.*

There was consternation in the club on Sunday when the hypnotist dropped the microphone on his foot. The scenes that followed his single word expletive defy description.

It was nice to see our Treasurer again last week and I would like to take this opportunity to thank the Prison Authorities.

Some of the audience complained about the quality of the juggling act but I told them that it was out of my hands.

I must insist that committee members, in future, stop using fictitious names when they sign for their expenses. You couldn't make it up!

The girl singer was very nice and her measurements, she told me, were 38-24-38. Unfortunately, not in that order.

The 2-minute respectful silence for Tommy Houghton was completely ruined by him shouting that members should wait until he's dead.

THE TRUTH BEHIND

'THE ORIGINAL ALTON DOUGLAS'

Joan Armatrading, a fine artiste, fellow-Brummie, singer/guitarist and 3-time Grammy Award nominee, was due to record a half hour programme in 1977, for BBC Midlands TV. Sadly, due to an extended tour in Switzerland, she had to drop out. The producer, John Clarke, asked if Gordon Stretch and I could fill the gap. Warning bells should have sounded! With only a few days to go, we cobbled together four sketches, a solo spot for me, music by the excellent jazz band of Tommy Burton and a brief appearance by my friend, the comic, Don Maclean.

A meagre two hours of studio time were allotted, Peter Brookes, who was a regular in *Crossroads* at the time, and Anne Beverley were recruited. The director was summoned out of retirement. One problem was that the band could not read music and my big number was an impression of Topol singing *If I Were A Rich Man* from the musical, *Fiddler On The Roof.* Somehow, they coped.

The Original Alton Douglas went out the following Friday. It was a disaster! There was a slight fault on the sound and it was just a dreadful quickly put-together mish-mash. The critics moved in and not only was it not the success we had all hoped for but the organiser who had booked me for a cabaret at the prestigious Penns Hall Hotel cancelled!

(That experience taught me that, round every corner, there is a waiting banana skin!)

Forty five years later, Kaleidoscope, an organisation that stores classic television programmes, including most of Bob Monkhouse's archive, asked me if I had a copy of the show and could they borrow it for copying purposes. My answers were 'Yes' and a resounding 'No!'

Fortunately, John Clarke realised we were not solely to blame and shortly afterwards, Gordon and I co-wrote three series of *Know Your Place*, with me as the quizmaster. It was the biggest success BBC TV in the Midlands had ever had, pulling in two million viewers every week – an unheard-of number for an opt-out programme. Into gaol – out of gaol!

ALL OVER THE PLACE

A Scottish shopkeeper, who wore his sporran inside his kilt, was arrested by police today for fiddling with his change.

As the rush to be the first in the advertising market intensifies, this Xmas, the Government have said that Santa will be delivering Easter eggs and hot cross buns.

The price of seats for West End shows has reached such astronomical proportions that some ticket offices have decided to double as pawnbrokers.

The collision, between a McDougall's flour van and a van containing theatrical wigs, has resulted in a series of self-raising, hair-raising problems.

The Royal Navy intercepted a Russian submarine in the Thames earlier today. The Captain said that it was all a big mistake – he wasn't sure if it was left or right at Vladivostok.

The price of milk has risen dramatically this winter, and cows at one Dorset farm are on strike, demanding a substantial increase in their silage supply.

Due to global warming, the ex-igloo dwellers in Greenland are insisting that it should be renamed 'Lakeside'.

In America, it has been announced, for the first time, that the annual Thanksgiving Day has been replaced by a 'What-The-Hell-Can-Go-Wrong-Next Day?'

Following the dramatic reduction in the police budget, the entire panoply of panda cars has been sold off. In future, all speeding cars will be pursued by an elderly constable on a push bike, shouting, 'Hey, you, I'll tell your mother.'

NEW YEARS EVE AND

RATTLING PETE ROADWORKS

New Year's Eve can be the ultimate nightmare for most musicians and acts. The date seems to give conditions and the audience a licence to show their worst sides.

The first one I did, with my quartet, was in a cavernous room the size of two football pitches. We placed our three microphones at stage front, with four from their sound system and we still weren't loud enough. Afterwards, the organiser said, 'You were very good, lads, but you could have played a bit louder.'

-.-.-.-

Most early band bookings were weddings. In those days, a taxi firm, florist or photographer would visit the groom's home beforehand, at the same time recommending other services. Photographer Peter Heath passed on dozens of jobs. Some years later, I learned he was now a country and western singer called 'Yodelling Pete Kingsway'. The least I could do was book him, only to find he was an excellent act. One New Year's Eve, we found ourselves at the Watercourse restaurant, in Stourbridge. The audience was exactly as expected. I did three or four gags, couldn't be heard and introduced Pete. He did three songs and reintroduced me, and so it went on for ninety minutes of pure purgatory. The owner was delighted. 'That was great – can I book you both again for next year, please?' Guess our response.

(As a joke, and I have no idea why, I renamed him 'Rattling Pete Roadworks'. I even threatened to introduce him as that!)

-.-.-.-

A Chesterfield club's contract insisted I arrive at 7pm. Knowing how late these jobs normally were, for the only time in my career, I dawdled and arrived 20 minutes late. The Club Chairman was pacing up and down outside. 'Where have you been? We put the show on at 8 so our members can get home before the drunks are on the roads!' That was the only New Year's Eve job I ever enjoyed – and I was home before midnight.

SECOND THOUGHTS

A few old sayings have literally gone into the language over the years, but I can give you an insight into what the scribes actually muttered under their breaths:

'Don't spend what you don't have.' (Spend something someone else doesn't have).

'Actions speak louder than words.' (But always pray your opponent is short sighted).

'Neither a borrower nor a lender be.' (Not the best advice for an aspiring young bank manager).

'It's always best to get it off your chest.' (Unless you're a knight in full armour in the middle of a battle.)

'Better late than never.' (If it's a speeding train and you are tied to the track, then that would not be the preferred option.)

'The pen is mightier than the sword.' (Try telling that to a marauding pirate.)

'No man is an island.' (The Isle of Man?)

'Put your money where your mouth is.' (Not recommended by a speech therapist.)

'When one door closes, another one opens.' (Always give it a push, just in case.)

'There's no such thing as a free lunch.' (Then explain luncheon vouchers.)

'What's done is done.' (How about that for stating the obvious?)

FROM THEN UNTIL NOW

Zulu and *Zulu Dawn* have always been two of my favourite films but my interest has been heightened, over the years, by the date. The British invasion force suffered one of their greatest defeats at Islandlwana but, later in the day, one of their greatest victories at Rorke's Drift. The date was 22nd January 1879. On that date, I was, exactly to the day, minus 59 years old!

-.-.-.-

When I started at Saltley Grammar School in 1948, I followed in the footsteps of my cousin Ruby and my brother Maurice, both of whom were pupils there in the 30s. The maths teacher, Mr Cooke, seeing my details on the list and remembering my predecessors, said to Maurice, some years later when they met up, 'I thought "Good God, there's three of them!" '

-.-.-.-

All through my years at the school I was at the bottom of the lowest class every term. Somehow, I never clicked into a real learning mode. The only other person I can find who almost matches my lack-of scholastic-skills was my hero – Sir Winston Churchill!

-.-.-.-

Maurice, by this time, was a football referee and one of his friends was a fellow-ref, Mr Southern, another of the teachers at Saltley. For some reason, my brother was convinced that I was a good cricketer (I was keen but never good). Knowing that the teacher was responsible for one of the teams, he somehow persuaded him to book me for the Second XI. After a score of 1 followed, in the next game, by a first ball duck, Mr Southern said to him, 'I'm sorry, Maurice, but not even for a good friend!'

-.-.-.-

In Germany, in 1958, as a member of the band of the 5th Royal Inniskilling Dragoon Guards, I sang, in partnership with Bill Briggs, a couple of song parodies that we had written. The announcer on that BFN (British Forces Network) broadcast was Chris Howland. To our surprise, the following year, Chris, who was by no means a singer, recorded his own song *Fraulein* and had quite a hit with it. Apparently, the German public loved his fractured version of their language.

-.-.-.-

On to my cabaret days, a Stratford-on-Avon hotel cancelled my booking the night before. With no chance of filling the date, I made a formal complaint to Equity. I appeared in the Small Claims Court with union rep Eddie Wyatt, who was told by the District Judge, 'I give judgement in your favour but Mr Wyatt, you have both had a wasted journey. If you had checked before you left Wales and Mr Douglas left Birmingham, you would have been told that the hotelier has no money whatsoever.'

-.-.-.-

I arrived to speak at a ladies' luncheon club, in Stourbridge, and immediately recognised the Chairperson. With my quartet, I had played for her birthday party on a luxury barge. When she stood up to introduce me, she began with, 'Ladies, I had Alton for my 21st birthday (loud laughter). No, what I mean is that I had Alton and his band - (gales of laughter).' Flustered, she hurried through the rest of my intro. I opened with, 'Well, I have to apologise for those words. When she said that she had me and my band – whatever you are thinking – you are right.'

-.-.-.-

Over the years, with my quartet, we played at the quayside to welcome returning ships, on several barges and on one or two mixed versions of floating vessels. It is a good job that we never had any difficulties because not only can I not swim but I can't even paddle successfully.

One event that was no joke - at a dinner at the Botanical Gardens in Birmingham, I was the Guest Speaker. The self-important Toastmaster took so long over my introduction that sections of the audience started booing him. Completely unperturbed, he kept going until they started catcalling him - it wasn't until then that this vainglorious fool concluded his monologue. Now then, you try and make an audience laugh, all of whom think that you requested that tiresome introduction.

(If I still sound bitter, after all these years, it's because I have no part in my life for that kind of vanity.)

-.-.-.-

2022 saw the publication of our 65th book. Some years before, I had become a Facebook friend with Tim Harnden-Taylor, an ex-Black and White Minstrel. Over the years, he wrote a series of articles about his walks, seen through the eyes of the family dog. I cajoled him into finding a publisher. He contacted Penny Reeves, the author of *Mitchell Magic* (the biography of the Minstrels' founder George Mitchell). Penny, by this time, had her own company, Saron Publishers. This resulted in three excellent books, *The Meanderings of Bing, The Ramblings of Bing* and *The Ruminations of Bing.* Knowing that my regular publisher, Brewin Books Ltd, was now specialising in history books, I sent a rough copy of *I Look At It Like This* to her and it appeared in print last Xmas – greatly polished by Penny.

THE AGENT CALLED

Artistes would occasionally recount disparaging tales about their agents. Far be it from me to join the chorus.

'He's a sentimental man. If his wife died, he would insist on keeping 10% of her ashes.'

-.-.-.-

'I'm terribly sorry I had to miss that booking last week but I was stuck in hospital at the time.'

'Don't worry about it, just send the commission.'

-.-.-.-

'He said, "I know the club's got a bad reputation, but you just can't believe everything you read in hospital reports." '

-.-.-.-

'If he arrived in Hell, he'd want to know who had the fuel concession.'

-.-.-.-

'That comic he booked last week – his jokes were so old they paid him in groats.'

-.-.-.-

'Someone in the office got a bit confused. The rugby club got the Mozart String Quartet and the Catholic Club had two strippers and a blue comic.'

-.-.-.-

'I reckon he gets a monetary backhander from these clubs. Me, I'd like to just give him a backhander.'

-.-.-.-

'He sent his finance officials round to collect the money I owed him. I counted four of them before I lost consciousness.'

QUESTIONS YOU HAVE LONGED TO ASK

Do all newcomers to the circus workforce have to swear allegiance to the clown?

How many mathematicians does it take to change a light bulb? Difficult to sum up.

Did the man who first operated the lie detector have to take a lie test first?

Do professional dog walkers ever stop for a cat nap?

Do you remember that woman's voice on the Speaking Clock? I wonder if she ever had to ring herself up to check the time?

When road workers have an argument, do they have to patch things up to cement their relationship?

How long does it take council office employees to change a light bulb? By the time they receive written approval and a bulb, they are probably all used to using torches.

Does the Flat Earth Society ever organise trips around the globe?

When Christopher Columbus was wrongly accused of being the first man to discover the New World of the Americas, did he ever say, 'Well, I'm not taking the blame.'?

Have you ever noticed how AN Other seems to find his/her way, at some time, into every sporting side?

Why do the excerpts, on the flaps of dust jackets, always seem to be so much more exciting than the actual contents?

Do left-handed people always feel they are right?

If Twitter and Facebook joined forces, would they call it 'Twitface'?

How many television newsreaders does it take to change a light bulb? Impossible to do without the aid of autocue.

When the Highways Department have to use up their budget before the end of the financial year, why do they always spend it digging up our road?

If too many cooks spoil the broth, would not enough make it any better?

When the Berlin Wall came down, do you think any of the husbands said, 'Isn't that nice, dear? Now your mother can just pop over to see us any time she likes.'?

Do corkscrew manufacturers ever feel they have been twisted?

How many pilots does it take to change a light bulb? Only one as long as they are guaranteed a safe landing.

Do caravan owners get the uneasy feeling that they are being followed?

Do Sumo wrestlers have to weigh up their opponents?

I wonder if tortoises think, 'I must have paid the mortgage off on this place by now'?

How many footballers does it take to change a light bulb? It could take all eleven but they would need extra time.

Do librarians ever think, 'Hey, I was just going to borrow that book!'?

Do people who spend their days texting ever realise that they are actually using a phone?

Why do colouring books include pictures of pandas or piano keyboards or zebra crossings?

Do comedians ever feel the urge to say, 'You should see me with a live audience!'?

With so many comedic topics being *infra dig*, do you think that the straight man has the best job?

Do light bulb manufacturers get really fed up with all these terrible jokes about their product?

WHY CAN'T I BE A TORTOISE?

If only life had taught us
To live as simply as the tortoise.
He's actually a kind of Romany
That travels in his little home and he
Lives on things like healthy lettuce
And I'd like to place an even bet his
World spins happily on its axis
Without paying a mortgage or ordering taxis.

CURIOS

My birth date, 22nd January, was also shared by a lot of other people:

Francis Bacon: 1st Viscount St Alban. English philosopher and statesman.
DW Griffith: American film director. Considered to be one of the most influential in motion picture history.
Walter Raleigh: Statesman, soldier and explorer. Certainly one of the most notable Elizabethan characters.
Alf Ramsey; Football player, Captain and later Manager of England's national side.
Oh, and by the way, Queen Victoria died on 22nd January 1901.

Jo, 1st August, also had famous connections – regal and tonsorial:

Emperor Go-Komatsu: The 100th Emperor of Japan.
Yves St Laurent: The famous French hair stylist/designer.

You might also find it difficult to get through your day without being aware of these facts:

It snows in the Sahara – it used to be, at one time, a lush rain forest.
You cannot hold your nose and hum at the same time.
France is the most visited country in the world.
The first vacuum cleaner was a horse-drawn petrol power unit and houses were cleaned from the outside.
King Charles III has inherited most of the country's swans.
Everyone is taller first thing in the morning.
Film Director Alfred Hitchcock was an Ovophobe – someone frightened of eggs.
A quarter of our bones are in our feet.

There are hundreds of other startling facts - but you have probably suffered enough by now!

MORE NEWS FROM THE LOCALE

I have just renewed my driving licence at 70. With the cost of petrol these days, I can barely afford the free licence.

The ginger Tom next door chases everything in the neighbourhood but never catches anything. Neither does his cat.

The petition concerning the closure of the local police station has been rejected by the authorities. It will remain open.

The new supermarket on the corner of High Street and Price Road has undergone a change of name. The management felt that the combination of the two names was conveying the wrong message – the 'High Price Store'.

Our opticians' has had to close since the manager said that he didn't feel they could see their way through the recession.

The local MP was around a while ago, reassuring everyone that his party has a firm grip on the nation's finances – the collecting boxes will be arriving next week.

A team of sniffer dogs has been sent in to one of our local burger bars to sniff out any traces of beef.

The traffic calming measures appear to be working in New Road. The council say that they will remove the gun emplacement in a week.

A lot of residents have complained about the music in the library so, from next week, there will be a full-time rapper instead of Mr Milton and his records.

The winter of 1947 was just as bad as they say. I remember seeing the School Board man going round to the headmaster's house and frogmarching him through the snow to the school.

A WRITER'S LOT

Being a writer of humorous material can be a very satisfying business but at times, believe me, it can produce some equally funny reactions!

No one ever believes that jokes originate anywhere – but I can promise you that they do! I started writing them at the age of 13 and mine have appeared, not only in comics' acts but also in newspapers, magazines, radio programmes and even some years ago I read one on the back of a matchbox!

-.-.-.-

I wrote some gags for a Birmingham comedian's appearance on the talent show *Opportunity Knocks*. Fifty years later, he still reckons the cheque is in the post.

-.-.-.-

A comic complained that he had heard one of the jokes in my book *Entertaining Thoughts* that he had just bought. I explained to him that, as I had been writing funnies for over seventy years, there was a possibility he could have. However, it did leave dozens and dozens he hadn't heard before. If he employed a writer today, a single joke would cost him over £10 - my book was £2.95!

-.-.-.-

Booked for a week's cabaret in a club, I arrived on the second night to find that the comic on before me was using most of my self-penned act. When I tackled him about it, he said 'I'm so sorry, I won't do it again – I knew I'd heard them somewhere before!'

-.-.-.-

I have been asked, so many times, in clubs and even by my own family, why I enjoy writing gags. Do you know, to this day, I haven't the faintest notion.

WELCOME TO THE CLUB

That doyen of the working men's clubs – the doorman – has always been my favourite clubland character.

'You'll have to put your car round the back, this way's for people.'

'Blimey, if I could afford a car like that, I wouldn't be working here.'

'If you're the comedian for tonight, you're not pinned up on the notice board.'

'The girl singer's already here. She's a big girl. I reckon she'll fill our stage.'

'You'll have to take your stuff through here - we can't afford a back door.'

(To a group with a van full of equipment) 'You won't need that lot in here – we've got a microphone.'

'How many of you are there in the group? We don't get this many in the audience.'

'The acts go round the back here unless they're affiliated.'

'A word of advice if you're the comedian. Don't crack too many jokes, the Chairman's just lost his wife.'

'No, mate, the British Legion's down the road. It's the one with the police cars outside.'

'You've been here before – I thought you had – I never forget a duff act.'

(On the way out) 'Nice to see you again. I remember all them jokes from the last time you were here.'

REMNANTS FROM THE WEST END

During my stint in the West End, in the late 60s, the management team who looked after my work, knowing my love of Jewish humour, used to constantly feed me jokes. Being Jewish themselves, Bertie Green, Harry Dawson and Dave Froms helped me to fill up more than one notebook.

One sunny afternoon Bertie reckoned he was stopped by someone in the street who said, 'I'm trying to get somebody to help me out.' Bertie looked at him, 'I must say you've chosen a lovely day for it.'

'Can I help them out? Every day, I'm asked for a handout. Why me? I've told them I've got nothing and every day, little of that.'

Dave told me a monkey went into his brother's sandwich bar and asked for, 'A lean corned beef sandwich on rye.' Dave's brother said, 'You're the first monkey I've ever had in here.' The monkey was indignant, 'I should think so at these prices!'

Harry came in one morning to announce that his wife had asked him, 'If you had your time, would you marry me again?' Harry thought for a moment, 'Probably – if I had to.'

'Papa, I don't want to go to England.'
'Stop complaining and keep swimming.'

'My wife accused me of being a poor loser. I said to her, "Did you ever see a rich one?" '

During the Six Day War, an Israeli soldier was trying to shoot one of the enemy. The Arab kept zig-zagging to get away from him. 'Hey, run in a straight line, you fool. These bullets cost money.'

One member of the audience at the Best Cellar, in Leicester Square, told me that he wanted on his headstone, 'I told Miriam my feet were killing me.'

THE FOLKS NEXT DOOR

His wife said she has trouble getting herself started every morning – personally, I don't think the anti-freeze was such a good idea.

They have so many disagreements their children have asked Amnesty International to mediate.

It started at the wedding when the vicar said to him, 'Do you take this woman ----? and he replied, 'Would you?'

I've heard of being cautious but the best man was a Marriage Counsellor.

At the reception the two families didn't exactly hit it off – well, actually, they did hit it off – but it was soon quelled by the Mounted Police.

I asked, at the time, if they'd both enjoyed the honeymoon. He looked puzzled, 'Both?'

I think she must have been somewhere hot recently because she's taken to sunbathing in the garden naked. I know that because their neighbour, on the other side, has just sold his binoculars.

She started getting out there first in the morning – it must be just a coincidence but the dawn chorus has suddenly developed laryngitis.

Things are far more peaceful, these days. At least we don't have to call the police out any more. Not since they put them on their daily rota.

There haven't been any problems with the kids for years either – it's quite a few years since they were packed off to Australia.

Anyway, I suppose, as neighbours go, I wish they would.

YOU ARE NUMBER 98 IN THE QUEUE

I managed to get an appointment at the doctor's today. It just took a while to get through the barbed wire, trip wires and the SS guards.

The receptionist had modelled herself on her favourite character. Attila the Hun.

You have to book your details in by entering your date of birth. I did and a note came up, 'And you are still with us?'

The doctor's manner could have been more welcoming. I sat down and he barked, 'Confess!'

'Doctor, I keep having these strange dreams. Last night, I dreamt I was a sofa.'
'Well, make yourself comfortable.'

'The night before, I was a filly running in the Oaks in the dark.'
'That's a nightmare.'

'I'll prescribe something for your wife to help you to sleep.'
'For my wife, Doctor?'
'Yes, it's a mallet.'

'Now I'm upset because she says she can read me like a book.'
'Well, what's wrong with that?'
'She can't stand the hero.'

'When do you want to see me again?'
'Preferably last week.'

'The doctor's arranging for me to see one of them occupational Terrapins.'
'I think you've got that wrong, Maisie, I think they are called Occupational Terrorists.'

ODDS AND SORTS

To most lads their dad is a hero and to this day mine is to me. During wartime Britain, he was the Deputy Head ARP Warden for Small Heath, a foreman at Castle Bromwich Aeroplane Factory, a Special Constable, a football referee and a husband and father to two sons. Is it any wonder that the Grim Reaper claimed him early? Seventy-five years later, he is still my Number One hero.

My dad was also a superb carpenter. An oak table, two wardrobes and an umbrella stand bear testimony to that. I am terrified to go near a hammer in case it takes it personally.

-.-.-.-

My family, over the years, have had several police connections. Dad was a Special, Uncle Ted was a fixture at Steelhouse Police Station and my nephew, John, was a Sergeant, just to mention a few. My only regular contact consisted of the number of times, as a comic, I was stopped by members of the thin blue line in the early hours. They always refused to let me go on my way until I told them a joke.

-.-.-.-

A relative passed away at the age of 92 and we were faced with the arduous task of clearing out the house. I have to say that the task was lightened somewhat when we discovered a box containing over two hundred Viagra tablets.

-.-.-.-

Jo's dad, badly injured in the First World War, was rushed into hospital. He always maintained that the blood transfusion service ran out of human blood and he was given horse blood. Several medics, over the years, have denied the possibility but nothing would deter him from that belief.

Going through her dad's possessions, Jo found a German luger and some bullets. Like most veterans I have met, he always refused to discuss any aspect of his military career and this is one more incident that remains a mystery to this day. How did he acquire them?

-.-.-.-

Children can be very cruel. We had a neighbour, Mr Swann, who, bearing in mind his name, had a very unfortunate waddle. We nicknamed him 'Bummy'. One afternoon, leading a string of kids, I crouched down and 'doing the walk', crept down beneath the level of his hedge and waddled past. There was a sudden angry roar and we realised he was about two feet away, trimming the hedge. There followed a string of words that none of us had ever heard before and I certainly didn't again until I encountered an Army Drill Sergeant.

-.-.-.-

During my National Service basic training days, the other recruits voted me the Politest Person and The Worst Soldier in the intake.

-.-.-.-

A friend of mine, off to see a theatre show, but running late, dashed out of the house, jumped on a bus and then suddenly realised he was wearing his reading glasses. He spent the entire evening reading the show.

-.-.-.-

One day I decided to treat a friend to a High Tea at the very swanky, very expensive Regents Park Hotel. The waiter said to him, 'And what would the young Sir like this afternoon?' My friend said, 'Beans on toast, mate?'

Ken Windsor was, at one time, a special constable. Patrolling the streets of Exeter, he slipped on a kerb in the main street just as a police car passed. One of his more helpful colleagues opened the window and with a megaphone, shouted, 'Get up, you lazy drunk.'

-.-.-.-

The family physician, Dr Davies, was quite a character. He opened the fridge in his surgery, looked inside and gave a snort of disgust. 'I hate that, when irresponsible people don't replace things!' He stomped off to the door, turned to me and said, 'There's only me goes in that fridge!'

-.-.-.-

I was stopped by a man and woman in the street. He said, 'Hey, do you remember me?' I said, 'I do, you used to live just across from us in Small Heath and you are just about the same age as me.' He shook his head. 'I've just bought your biography and you didn't mention me.' I paused for a moment. 'Well, I couldn't think of anything favourable to say. The only thing I could remember is that you were renowned for expelling large amounts of air from your person.' His wife chimed in, 'Oh, he still does that!'

-.-.-.-

Our friend, Sheila Thompson, going on holiday to Mijas in Spain, decided to take a Birmingham book with her to show a resident. She walked into the hotel breakfast room with the book in her hand, to hear one of the guests say to her, 'Excuse me, is that an Alton Douglas book?' Sheila was surprised, 'How could you possibly know that? You said yesterday that you were from Aberdeen.' He replied, 'I was in Birmingham last year and I bought two of his books.'

SCHOOL DAZE

Absenteeism was always a problem at our school, particularly amongst the teachers.

The major setback was the Head Teacher. He was missing so often they issued him with a visitor's badge.

The school's honour board was so small it was used as a keyhole draught excluder.

Our Maths teacher told me he was 101% sure I would end up as a derelict.

The teacher in charge of the fire drill was delighted. He said he had never seen such flames.

Due to cutbacks the Christmas party was suspended until the summer and the Head said that the annual outing would be postponed until Hell freezes over.

School dinners were so bad that, when they asked if anyone wanted 'Seconds', nobody wanted 'Firsts'.

There were so many religions at Assembly that prayers were replaced by a house of Bingo.

'What makes you think you are qualified to be our swimming instructor?'

'Sir, I've got webbed feet.'

'That'll do.'

He was one of those teachers who had absolutely nothing to say and insisted on saying it.

The school magazine has now progressed to words AND pictures.

I understand that chalk and slates have recently been replaced by pencils and paper.

I had to stand outside for misbehaving so regularly that my schooling must have suffered, but I always had a lovely suntan.

I was there in the 50s and I've been told that some teachers, from that time, may shortly be offered early retirement.

The History teacher thought that 1066 was the time that the Battle of Hastings started.

The Geography teacher tried to convince us that Ben Nevis was a close personal friend.

I don't think he was really suited to the job. He had to use a compass, each night, to find his way home.

It was a silly idea to have woodwork and cookery lessons in quick succession. One pupil went home and roasted a wooden joint.

Sports Day was ruined when the Games Master swallowed his whistle, coughed and simultaneously started five races.

The idea of 'back squadding' pupils, until they attained a certain academic standard, was finally abandoned when Billy Whittaker collected his pension for the first time.

I saw a very elderly man in the street yesterday and thought, 'I'm sure he used to be our oldest teacher.' I said, 'Excuse me, but weren't you a teacher at my old school?' He looked very annoyed. 'No, you fool, I used to sit next to you!'

The police went to the school last week to break up a hooligans' fight. Several teachers were arrested.

'What makes you think you'll make a good French teacher?'
'Sir, I've seen *Monsieur Hulot's Holiday* three times.'
'That'll do.'

My favourite was the Science teacher. He was always experimenting with explosives. I don't know exactly what happened to him but we heard a good report.

THE SECRET

Keep this secret
Under your hat,
If possible
Under your hair.
Seal your lips,
(But do take care)
Mumble in French
If necessaire.

Don't give clues
Don't even sketch me.
Write in codes
Purloined from Bletchley.

It can't appear
In any casebook
And certainly not
On Twitter or Facebook.

Wrap it up
In a duffel coat,
Don't give enemies
Chance to gloat.

On second thoughts,
Don't ask me how,
I've completely forgotten,
What it was by now

THE ONLOOKER HEARS

MOST OF THE GAME

From an early age, a percentage of my income has always been allotted to stocking up with notebooks and pencil/pens. I cannot remember a time when they have not occupied an important place in my pockets. Now, in later life, they are proving to be invaluable as I trawl through them to find treasures that have amused me over the years. I don't think anyone, in the accommodation I inhabited as a musician or comic, ever suspected that their comments would achieve immortality!

'There's always one, isn't there? He sits at the front, looking thoroughly fed up and uninterested. Anybody would think he was there under sufferance. Last night, it was my agent.'

-.-.-.-

'The Entertainment Secretary said, "Your group is too loud for this room." I said to him, "I should tell them all to switch their hearing aids off then!" '

-.-.-.-

'I asked the barman if he could tell me the best way to get back to the digs.' He said, "Blimey, mate, I wouldn't be in a rush to get back there!"

-.-.-.-

'I've told the agent that if he books me back at that club again, I'll report him to the League Against Cruel Sports.'

-.-.-.-

'It was their Chairman's Night last night. I watched them at the free buffet. I think they ate the table.'

'I'm thinking of retiring from the clubs. Yesterday, I could have retired halfway through my act and nobody would have noticed.'

-.-.-.-

'Do you think these digs ever have any heating on? I could swear that last night I met the Abominable Snowman on the landing. He reckoned he was going out into the garden for a warm.'

-.-.-.-

'My manager and agent are taking so much of my earnings, it would be cheaper to pay them not to book me.'

-.-.-.-

'Do you reckon the landlady's cutting down on our meals? I'm sure tomorrow, she'll ask me for my ration book.'

-.-.-.-

'Talk about working with dep musicians – the only one in the band I recognised last night was me.'

-.-.-.-

'Somebody told me, "Come to the North East, the clubs are friendlier." The clubs might be, it's the members I have trouble with.'

-.-.-.-

'The Concert Secretary said, "With the girl singers, I look for three spots." I was very indignant. I retorted, "I think you've found two of them already." '

The tales of requesting directions to various venues were highly amusing if, at times, I suspect, a bit far-fetched. I am still amazed that musos and artistes ever found their way about.

'This bloke said if I dropped him off at work, he could take me there when he'd finished.'

-.-.-.-

'I'm sure the instructions he gave me were spot on. The only trouble is that I don't speak fluent Serbo-Croatian.'

-.-.-.-

'I thought to myself, "If I could only find a policeman." In the end, I got so confused looking for one, I thought, "I'll wait till I get to the club and ask them where I can find one!" '

-.-.-.-

'Just my luck to get a bad-tempered copper. When I asked him the way to Middlemore Club, he said, "Don't ask me, do I look like a traffic cop?" '

-.-.-.-

'One bloke waved his arms about so much, a man on the other side of the road, came over and asked if he could place a bet.'

-.-.-.-

'I've decided it would be simpler to buy an A-Z of all the major cities and towns. The smaller ones, I'll just buy an A-B.'

FROM CITIZEN SMITH TO THE PINK PANTHER

In 1968 I was the warm-up comic for the first series of the sit-com *Citizen Smith*, in which Peter Vaughan played Charlie Johnson, the father-in-law of Wolfie (Robert Lindsay). He said to me, during a break in rehearsals, 'It's a nuisance - people keep mistaking me for Robert Shaw!' Try as I might, even to this day, I can't see the vaguest resemblance.

-.-.-.-

During the course of my weeks on the show, I became friendly with Mike Grady. He played Ken Mills, Wolfie's mate. As I mentioned in *I Look At It Like This,* he invited me to see him in *Once Upon A Catholic*, at Wyndhams Theatre, where I met a fellow-Brummie, Jeff Rawle, (best known for his part in *Drop The Dead Donkey*). Mike himself is best remembered as 'Barry' in *Last Of The Summer Wine* but if you want to catch him in tip-top slapstick form, you need to see him in *Return Of The Pink Panther*, as a bell boy caught innocently with Peter Sellers in a bedroom scene. That is farce playing at its very best.

Mike and I are still in touch today.

-.-.-.-

John Taylor, my friend from Harborne in Birmingham, was Peter Sellers' understudy on all the Pink Panther films. He said that Sellers told him that the Clouseau accent, the make-up and his entire appearance (including that memorable moustache) were entirely of his own devising.

-.-.-.-

John wrote a book *Love, Cricket, Peter Sellers* and, although he gave me a copy of it, like so many things, it has disappeared into that Bermuda Triangle that everyone seems to have in their home. I'm sure you know what I mean. Objects that you value, and wouldn't dream of getting rid of, take it on themselves to go walkies.

HOME IS WHERE

I HANG MY HEAD

I didn't realise there was a damp course in the house, until I saw a tutor carrying his files and computer in.

My wife loves the dampness. Strange, she also encourages me to call her 'Ducky'.

It is a bit draughty too, I suppose. The Meteorological Office has just asked if they can use it as a wind tunnel.

Still, we are getting a new roof next week. To be precise, it's our first.

The semi-detached houses are very small and tightly packed together in our street. I hadn't noticed until the man next door asked me if I'd mind moving up the sofa a bit.

Their house is an absolute pigsty. The pigs don't seem to complain very much.

I thought the Health Inspector was trying to be Christmassy when he said he liked the pigs' blankets.

The people opposite aren't exactly presentable. I see they've even had the dog tattooed.

That dog is supposed to be a guard dog. He's not what I would call effective – he lets their family in.

Anyway, Mum's made our house completely sound-proof. She's made Dad take a vow of silence.

Mind you, his language is very bad. When he went into the confessional, the priest had to ask for an interpreter.

The house is on the market now. Well, no estate agent would even consider handling it.

ACTING UP

IN BIRMINGHAM

Being a proud Brummie, I thought it appropriate to list some of the actors who have come from our city. Space precludes me listing all their appearances and achievements, so I thought I would mention just a few.

Alan Napier: Kings Norton born, he is most famous for his part as butler Alfred Pennyworth in the US Batman series.

-.-.-.-

Tony Britton: He was born in an upstairs room at the Trocadero pub, in Temple Street. His dad eventually was the licensee of seven different public houses. He appeared in numerous film and TV parts, including one of my favourite war films, *Operation Amsterdam.*

-.-.-.-

Martin Shaw: Brought up in Erdington and Sutton Coldfield, he appeared in fifty-seven episodes of *The Professionals.* Recently, he played the name part in *Inspector George Gently.* His estimated worth is just over £20 million.

-.-.-.-

Barry Jackson: He came from Longbridge where his father worked at the Austin factory. Best known for his role as the pathologist in *Midsomer Murders*, starring John Nettles.

-.-.-.-

Annette Badland: Originating from Edgbaston, by a strange twist of fate she also became a pathologist in *Midsomer Murders.*

-.-.-.-

David Harewood: His parents came from Barbados and settled in Small Heath. His first film role was in *The Hawk*, since when he has become quite a big star. In 2007, he donated his bone marrow to save the life of a patient.

FUNNY FOLK

The Red Indian who couldn't tell the difference between heads and tails collected some very funny scalps.

The Jewish hotel detective went round pounding on doors and shouting, 'Have you got a ham in there?'

She applied for a Government apprenticeship as a test pilot for chastity belts.

The bank manager who wouldn't agree to an extraction until the dentist had completed a withdrawal form.

My niece was tattooed around the corner – the only trouble is that she can't see it without using a mirror.

He was someone who would complain about everything. He rented a room in a bungalow and then moaned about the noise from the people upstairs.

My wife complains about me playing the drums at three in the morning. How unreasonable is that! Do I complain about her sleeping?

He decided it wasn't such a good idea to open a shop specialising in repairing air guitars.

'Honestly, her neckline was so low she spilled herself all over her drink.'

I wanted to be a mountaineer but the problem is that I get giddy climbing the kerb.

If you want to see nature in the raw, just go to any park. I've seen people doing things in public I've never wanted to do in private.

He resigned from the darts club when they wouldn't allow him on the board.

Following a cyber-attack on the UK telephone system, the police are asking anyone with information to please ring 998.

My brother is so religious he wears stained glass contact lenses on Sundays.

He once tried racing greyhounds but, unfortunately, they couldn't find his size in muzzles.

The dating service offered to match him up with a Red Cross nurse but he said he preferred the pink friendly ones.

My tailor can make you a suit that fits like a glove. If you want one that fits like a suit ...

My last suit cost over £500. If you don't believe me, I can show you the summons.

A man was arrested in Leicester Square for shouting, 'All politicians are crooks!' He was fined £100 for being a public nuisance and £50 for a breach of the Official Secrets Act.

'Doctor, what do you think is the matter with me?'

'I don't know, it must be the drink.'

'What shall I do then?'

'Come back when I'm sober.'

His hearing isn't very good these days. When he talks to himself, he has to keep saying, 'Pardon?'

She couldn't make up her mind whether to be the person in charge of land fill projects or an archaeologist. It resulted in her filling up holes faster than she could find the sites.

LETTERS AFTER MY NAME

Determined to make my mark on history,
Almost since I emerged from the womb,
Today I solemnly carved my initials
On the side of a Pharoah's tomb.

COLD CALL

I have to climb out from my bath,
The perfect place to lie and read in.
The phone has rung, some man would like
To fit some windows I don't need in.

FISH DISH WISH

I'm sorry to say it's just our luck,
The chippy's now a complete disgrace.
Tonight I find I'm firmly stuck
Between a rock and a very hard plaice.

SEEKER OF TRUTH

Some see me as a nonconformist,
A pillar of wisdom, their main informist.
I try to show them wrong from right,
What might not be and then what might.
While others seek my wise advice,
(I hear some comments shrewd and nice.)
The family says from here to Lydiate,
I'm the champion village idiot.

THE RAMBLINGS OF A HACK

Back to reality. I thought you might like to see a couple of Showbiz articles I wrote in my 1970s' fortnightly columns for a Birmingham newspaper.

KNOWING MY PLACE

'How do you go about putting together a television show?' With the regular Tuesday night BBC1 TV programme *Know Your Place* now going into the semi-final stage and yours truly being seen each week as the quizmaster, I thought I'd let you into a few trade secrets. The young, go-ahead producer, John Clarke, was assigned to look after his brainchild and he in turn (with a sudden rush of blood to the head) decided that a comedian would be the person to keep it all light-hearted. John and I had previously worked together so we knew what we were letting ourselves in for.

It seemed a good idea, in order to contribute something more than a parrot-like reading of the questions, if I were to become involved in the research for the programme too. So, armed with the list of chosen towns, a few pages torn from one of my old school exercise books and a freshly sharpened pencil, I set off in mid-June to tour the Midlands.

VAULTS

I aimed first of all for the curators of the museums, the chief librarians and the local newspapers. At the same time, my permanent co-writer, Gordon Stretch, was buried deep in the vaults of the Birmingham libraries (served him right too).

I also pestered the museum staffs to loan out objects that I hoped would puzzle our contestants more than somewhat.

Running parallel with our efforts, *Pebble Mill at One* loaned us one of their researchers, Heather Turner, and she, in cahoots with Rotarians, Round Table organisations etc, shortlisted local characters.

Finally after some good natured banter, three contestants emerged, looking very battle-scarred and bewildered, to represent their town. We also traipsed around cobbled streets and looked for suitable oddities to be photographed.

Meanwhile, back at the Beeb, captions were being prepared, music chosen, graphics illustrated and hearts broken. Several thousand script conferences were held and after much bartering between John, Gordon, our pretty director Kate Wright, the lovely Andrea and the Chairman, the final questions and a script resulted. Each contestant received instructions and every town held a reserve in readiness.

WARM-UP

On September 11, the first show between Hereford and Warwick took place. The drill now, as then, is for us to meet at 4 o'clock, have a dummy run with general questions and then at 6.45pm, go into the make-up room. With a few seconds for all the protagonists (and the rest of the half-hour for me), we stroll out wearing our new faces.

John and I set about 'warming-up' our small audience and at 7.30pm, it is all systems go. With stops and starts, we usually have a new victor by 8.15pm. Well, that's it! In the main, we concentrate on questions that would produce humorous or dramatic anecdotes and at all times, we endeavour to keep it light-hearted. If, at the end of our series, you know a bit more about eight Midland towns and in the process, you found the schooling fun, then we will have succeeded.

A FEW THOUGHTS FOR EASTER

Well, you can tell Christmas is nearly here with us - the shops are stocking Easter Eggs. Speaking of such things, some of the kids are so smart nowadays they're not hanging up stockings any more, they're hanging up pairs of tights. They're so blasé as well! One little boy shouted out early on Christmas morning, "Hey, Mum, tell Dad not to waste time putting on the fancy clothes. Just bring the toys in.'

My friend's an opportunist, though. Last year on Christmas Eve, there was a loud clap of thunder and quick as the following flash of lightning, he said, Don't expect too much this year, son - Santa's fallen off his sleigh.'

A GOLDEN SHOT

Last week, I had lunch with comedian Norman Vaughan and we were reminiscing over the days when you could put a fiver down to buy a coke and expect some change. Norman was appearing at the Alexandra Theatre with the touring company of *Calamity Jane* and he reminded me of an incident during the time I was the 'warm-up' comic for his *Golden Shot* programme.

I invited a woman out of our audience to come down on to the studio floor for a natter to see if she would be a suitable contestant for the show. She successfully clambered halfway down towards me, suddenly looked panic-stricken and dashed back to her seat.

Without so much as a fond farewell, she disappeared from sight. After what seemed an eternity, she reappeared looking very embarrassed and slowly descended to my level. 'What happened then?' She said, 'I'm sorry about that - I just realised I'd left my teeth in my handbag!'

Wednesday found me at the Sunnyside Restaurant in Northampton with ex-Seeker Lynn Paul. She has developed into a superb all-round artiste now and her 16-year-old sister also has a short feature in her act.

I finally managed a rare social evening at the Engine House, Tardebigge, to see the astounding international jazz guitarist, Barney Kessel. Wonderful!

ALTON'S ALTERNATIVE DICTIONARY

Once again I would like, in order to avoid any misunderstanding, to define certain words:

Assegai:	An indication that the correct person has been identified.
Behemoth:	A desire to be a member of a paraphyletic group of insects.
Commandeer:	The despairing cry of an impatient hubby.
Dachshund:	A well balanced domesticated carnivore, with a low centre of gravity.
Emmentaler:	A plethora of holes surrounded by cheese.
Fait Accompli:	Expression of smug self-satisfaction.
Gibberish:	A language mainly spoken by members of His Majesty's government.
Hooray Henry:	Someone who permanently thinks 'Three Cheers for Moi.'
Ignoramus:	A term used to describe a person who vehemently disagrees with you.
Jazzer:	A person who makes things up as they go along – another reference to a politician.
Kendo:	A Scotsman agreeing to do a task.
Levee:	Posh word for a toilet.
Microwave:	A timid recognition with a minimal amount of hand movement.

Nudity:	For anyone with a short memory trying to remember how they looked before dressing.
Osmosis:	An Australian prophet.
Pizza:	A meal consisting of an ill-judged assortment of foodstuffs on a decidedly indigestible base.
Quadrangle:	A four sided argument.
Rigmarole:	An attempt, by an actor, to persuade the Producer to improve their role.
Semi-conductor:	A part-timer in charge of an orchestra.
Tambourine:	An instrument that requires beating, along with the player.
Umbrella:	A protective weather device that distinguishes the male upper crust from us rain-soaked cap wearers.
Ventriloquism:	The art of saying almost anything to yourself without getting arrested.
Wapentake:	The act of being hit over the head and at the same time being robbed.
Xylocarp:	A fish that plays a musical instrument.
Yuan Tan:	A remark concerning your recent sunbathing activities.
Z:	Indicates you have reached the end of the alphabet and your tether.

It seems to be almost sacrilege to make jokes about dictionaries - but you know me:

Incorrectly is spelt incorrectly. How can you trust the rest of it?

Somebody's stolen my dictionary and I'm at a loss for words.

My friend wanted to improve his language skills so I suggested he bought a dictionary. I asked him how he was getting on and he said, 'It was seriously boring. Such a big cast but what a terrible plot!'

He was so exasperated that he threw it at his wife. She retorted, 'Don't you use words like that with me!'

My brother bought a dictionary online and all the pages were blank. He said, 'Words fail me.'

Dictionaries are so predictable! Everything in them is in alphabetical order!

Before you open your dictionary to find a word to express your contempt, how about a little rhyme?

QUITE A SPELL

Whales are famous for their spout
That's all I wish to talk about,
Except my sense of humour fails
On seeing 'Wales' instead of 'Whales'.

WORK DETAILS

The only job I was fully qualified for read, 'No experience necessary.'

When I applied for a position at the gentlemen's outfitters, they asked me to send a photograph. Apparently, the manager said he hated her swimsuit.

I started on a Monday and finished on a Monday – by coincidence, it was the same day.

I went to the Job Centre so often they made me use the Tradesmen's Entrance.

One week, I was offered a job and my solicitor said that if I accepted, he could probably get me time off for good behaviour.

I did get a little office job. When I say' little', there were 3 of us and the office was so small we had to take it in turns to yawn.

I have no idea what we did and the boss was too shy to tell me.

Never did find out what sex the other person was either, they always had their back turned to me.

Anyway, I did eventually get a proper office job. The manager said, right off, he would give me a trial. I've no clue what I did wrong.

The second week I was promoted. I was put solely in charge of counting the paper clips.

I think I may be okay here. I've just been told that my work has to be seen to be believed.

Just to establish our credentials. Our family goes back to the dawn of ages. I'm not sure if that's the pub on the corner or the landlady's name.

Dad worked in a bakery as a smelter. It was his job to say, 'Smelt as if it was burning to me.'

He was brought up in a rough area where they would steal absolutely anything. For a while he was a rear gunner on a rubbish truck. Mum was the driver.

'Work' is a sacred word in our family, I have only ever heard it mentioned in a reverential whisper.

My brother was sacked from his job as an aeroplane mechanic – he would insist on bringing his work home with him.

No one realised until the stores recognised where the spare parts were being delivered.

The factory at the bottom of our road finally reopened yesterday, after a month, when the boss remembered where he'd left his keys.

They make jigsaw puzzles – all the workers are on piecework. The management say they may be able to make it full time when they get the complete picture.

The original business folded in 1939 - as soon as they realised that there was a Nazi Party they had started producing paper hats.

For a while, there was an attempt at making various board games but they hadn't got a clue about Cluedo and someone else had the monopoly.

My brother is on the jigsaw puzzle assembly line but they reckon his face doesn't fit.

I don't know what Uncle Sid does but he must be an early riser. I heard Mum say he's up before the Judge.

His job must be important and quite dangerous. It seems to involve permanent nights and wearing a mask.

His wife is renowned for her charitable work. She constantly steals from the poor and gives to the rich.

She says it is second nature to her, being a Private Secretary to the Chancellor of the Exchequer.

Anyway, I have given up work for the last 20 years and I can't wait to retire.

THE RESTING ROO

I'd like to Introduce to you
The noble Mrs Kangaroo,
Whose claim to fame and please don't mock it.
Is possession of a massive pocket.
(To demonstrate I'm not a slouch
I know it should be called a pouch.)
Its raison d'être i.e. purpose:
Transporting babies and some surplus.
Amongst those objects, old and new,
The idle Mr Kangaroo.

THE NUMBER ONE FAN

I'm ready to own up
That now I'm a grown up
It's better than being a youth.
My trousers high-waisted,
My teeth dental-pasted,
I'm more than at home with the truth.
So I don't give a damn
(That's the way that I am.)
Decrepit and simply uncouth.

AGE CONCERNED

How did age descend on me
Like Newton's apple from the tree?
Why does posture of renown
Look like a question mark's in town?
And why's a head that once had hair
Almost baby's bottom bare?
Is it me? Am I to blame?
Or have you discovered much the same?

THE SOUND OF SILENCE

It may be a story,
It may be a rumour.
But I've heard of a man
With a sense of humour.
Perhaps in hotels.
Perhaps in pubs,
But it wasn't in any
Of the Northern clubs.

MY DEBUT AS A COMIC

My debut as a comic
Instead of the laughs a yawn or two
And to relieve the boredom a man in front
Set fire to his wife, as you do.

A shower of beer mats hit my knees
Followed by a pint of beer
But I managed to dodge an organ whistling
Tunelessly past my ear.

My debut as a comic
Almost caused a riot
But the committee agreed that I did succeed
In keeping the audience quiet.

HOT STUFF

A souvenir I've pinned up
Is a cartoon by Rowland Lindup
Depicting warm-up days
(Part of a comedic phase).
There's nothing remotely crazier
Than me on a burning brazier

JOG LOG

When I'm jogging every day
My breath expels in shortish pants
But in my fashion-conscious way
I'd never jog in shortish pants.

THE LINDUPS OF BLACKPOOL

OLD AMOS

Rowland Lindup (responsible for our cover picture) was a very talented Blackpool artist whose cartoons could be seen all over the city with many appearing on the South Shore's Pleasure Beach attractions. Along with that, he created Old Amos, an eagerly awaited addition to the monthly *Dalesman* magazine. Old Amos and his words of wisdom travelled the pages from 1953 to1989. When Rowland passed away his son, Pete, equally adept at the cartoonist's art, continued the tradition. It wasn't until the first payment arrived that Pete had to inform them the baton had passed to him. Now, 70 years later, Old Amos still tramples Yorkshire's streets.

A LIFE

Rowland and his brother, Norman, had not met up or spoken for several years so they decided to have a reunion. Sitting in his front room, Rowland said, 'Well, Norman, it's been a good number of years. What's happened to you in all that time?' Norman thought for a moment, sipped his tea, shuffled uneasily and then said, 'Nothing.'

ROMANCE IN THE AIR

Publicist George Bartram, with such clients as Morecambe and Wise, Tony Bennett and Ken Dodd, had to provide an attraction for the Euro Arts Exhibition, in Birmingham's Bingley Hall. He booked Rowland, with his canvas of a hundred top stars who had appeared in Blackpool over the years, to exhibit and discuss Showbiz with visitors. On his first night at the Holiday Inn, Rowland, unused to hotel life, forgot to lock his door. In the early hours, he heard the door open and a female voice whispered, 'Darling, it's only me.' He shot up in bed and let out a panic-stricken cry, 'I'm Rowland from Blackpool!' A hasty exit left behind just a whiff of expensive perfume.

THE GOLDEN SHOT

I was the warm-up comic for ATV's *The Golden Shot* for three years and on 17th June 1973, I was suddenly called in to host the show when regular compère Norman Vaughan lost his voice. Rowland, the next week, sent me the wonderful cartoon chosen for the cover of this book. It shows me sitting on a burning brazier to depict the warm-up aspect.

PETE MAKES AN IMPACT

Pete's grandpa, Fred, was the pit drummer at the Empire Palace, Dewsbury, from its 1909 opening to the final curtain in 1955, accompanying such artistes as 'Our Gracie' Fields, George Formby and Nat King Cole. For one Xmas he bought Pete a drum kit. Pete's first public engagement was at a church hall and halfway through his featured solo, the high hat and snare drum decided to collide with a mighty crash. Everything ground to a halt and after a slight pause, seven-year-old Pete said, 'Well, that's me buggered!' His mother, on piano, tried to crawl inside the instrument and Fred, sitting on the front row, almost collapsed with sheer delight.

MY FRIEND PETE

Incidentally, I did two lengthy summer seasons in revues at the South Shore Casino, in Blackpool, in 1969 and 1971 and Pete was part of the backing group. Together, we did a season with The Temperance Seven's show on Shanklin Pier in 1972, but, due to poor business, we seemed to spend more time in the box office and publicity-touring the island than we did performing. Our last summer season together was when I was the Principal Comic with the Fol-de-Rols at the De La Warr Pavilion, in Bexhill, in 1975.

For the last 50 years he has toured as a musical/comedy act (half music/half-wit). He also plays cornet or trombone with local jazz bands. We are still friends to this day.

I must be getting old. A chap in there put in a bid for me!

Rowland Lindup

One good thing about doing nowt is you can start anytime you feel like it!

Pete Lindup

MILITARILY SPEAKING

To me, military humour has always been a great source of delight. I'll spare you all but three examples of this:

ARMY

On an office wall, 'To all Officers - beware that your mouth doesn't operate faster than your brain.'

'If you can read this you are in range.'

'Beware of – well, just beware.'

AIR FORCE

'Sir, I was responsible for bringing down three aeroplanes.'
'What were you then? A rear gunner?'
'No, Sir, a mechanic.'

On a Naafi wall, 'Do not bring your parachute into these premises if it's open.'

And another wall, 'Keep flying – the alternative is a desk job.'

NAVY

'What would you do if an officer was swept overboard?'
'Depends on who it was, Sir.'

On a canteen wall, 'Beware if a Petty Officer ever says to you, "I was just thinking ..." '

My friend, Brian Caswell, reminded me of this order for storing torpedoes. 'It is necessary for technical reasons that these warheads be stored with the top at the bottom and the bottom at the top. So that there is no confusion as to which is the top and which is the bottom, for storage purposes, it will be seen that the bottom of each warhead has been labelled with the word TOP.'

THE TEACHER RIGHTS

I had some truly abysmal end-of-term school reports – many on a par with a few of these.

'He seems determined to be the school's Number One clown and I am equally determined that he will not beat me.'

'I am pleased to say that her truant days, this year, have so far exceeded my expectations.'

'His handwriting has improved to such an extent that I can now read all of his insults.'

'Mary spends so much time concentrating on the boys in the class, that I think she will either become a psychiatrist or a courtesan.'

'He has so many faults that writing his end-of-term reports has certainly improved my vocabulary.'

'She answers me back so often that I went home last night and shot my parrot.'

'I strongly recommend that you do not take this report home unless your parents have fire retardant furniture.'

'She cannot stop talking in the classroom and has all the makings of a natural politician.'

'He has been in trouble on such a regular basis that, this year, he has been given his own key to the Head Teacher's study.'

'It would be best, for the whole school, if he does not return again – we are already suffering severe staff shortages.'

THE TEACHER AS A SEER

It is not just us but quite a lot of celebrities had school reports that they must have been tempted to lose on the way home from school.

John Lennon: 'Certainly on the road to failure.'

-.-.-.-

Gary Lineker: 'He must devote less of his time to sport if he wants to be a success.'

-.-.-.-

Joanna Lumley: 'She must learn to speak politely when her requests are refused.'

-.-.-.-

Roald Dahl: 'An illiterate member of the class.'

-.-.-.-

David Bowie: 'He must learn that music will not make him a living wage.'

-.-.-.-

Judi Dench: 'She would be a very good pupil if she lived in this world.'

-.-.-.-

Richard Branson: 'He will either go to prison or become a millionaire.'

-.-.-.-

Sir Winston Churchill: 'In constant trouble to everybody and is always in scrapes. He cannot be trusted to behave himself anywhere.'

SHOWBIZ MISCELLANY No 1

Trail of the Pink Panther was a Peter Sellers film, constructed sometime after his demise. My friend, John Taylor, from Birmingham, his understudy for years, was used to link a lot of the action. So, when you watch it, just remember a lot of the time Peter is a lad from Harborne called John!

-.-.-.-

George Bartram, the Birmingham publicist, was also the agent responsible for most of my theatre bookings. He was asked to provide a name to open the Euro Arts Exhibition in the city's Bingley Hall. He contacted his old friend, actor Vincent Price, who, despite his film image, was actually a very affable man and entirely suitable for the event. Vincent immediately agreed and George thought that was that. However, just before the date, a film part came up and Vincent reluctantly had to cancel. George rang all his contacts and eventually the exhibition was opened by - the comedian Charlie Drake!

Unlikely as the substitution was, Charlie turned out to be a big hit and stayed there almost the whole of the day, talking to visitors and signing autographs.

-.-.-.-

Jane Asher came to Birmingham a few years ago to perform a shop opening. Jo and I chatted to her and I reminded her that we had met before. When I was at the Shakespeare Theatre Club, in Liverpool, with the Flowerpot Men and Wendy King, she and Paul McCartney came backstage to say 'Hello'. She was very gracious and gave Jo a little gift.

-.-.-.-

On one occasion, I was asked to compère an evening at the Grand Hotel in Birmingham. The Guest of Honour was to be Princess Margaret. As it was a cancer charity, a bright committee member wrote to her and asked if she would mind not smoking at the event.

We were a Guest of Honour short that night.

The thrill for me, that same evening, was that the Joe Loss Orchestra provided the music. In the interval, I chatted for twenty minutes with Joe. Just as in similar interludes with Peggy Lee, Stephane Grappelli and my Warwickshire cricketing hero, Tom Dollery, I can hardly recall one word!

-.-.-.-

Dennis Quilley was an actor I had always admired so I was pleased to see, when I read my script for *Murder of a Moderate Man*, that he was the lead actor. I was determined to tell him how much I'd enjoyed his portrayal *Privates on Parade*. Unfortunately, my one scene, as a Customs Officer boarding a plane, did not involve him. The nearest I got to appearing with him was when I stood behind him in the dinner queue. My admiration remained unexpressed.

-.-.-.-

Consulting my diary for September 1983, I was flabbergasted to find I had been the warm-up comic for something called *Mother Muffin's Music Stand*. No recollection of that at all! It wasn't until I read Victoria Wood's biography and it all came back. It was her first television programme and her guests were the Eagle Jazz Band. I remembered that she was so nervous before we started, that she lay flat on her back trying to relax! Just the start of a glorious career that ended far too early.

-.-.-.-

Like so many lads, one of my singing heroes in the 50s was Frankie Laine. So you can imagine the thrill when I was booked with him at the Cresta Club. Shortly after it was arranged, I learned I had been voted the Most Promising Comedian and would appear in the Midlands Variety Command Performance. Unfortunately, that too was at the Cresta, so my Laine week was cancelled.

To this day, I regret, ungratefully, that so many voted for me – I'd much rather have been on with Frankie Laine.

For many years I recorded literally hundreds of radio commercials – some with quite illustrious names, some with lesser-known but equally talented actors. However, the best ever was a seven-year-old boy who contributed, in one take, to a Xmas commercial. Nobody else was ever that good!

-.-.-.-

I was once involved in a marketing project in Birmingham, that necessitated interviewing people in the street. The first person I stopped was a woman struggling along the street, loaded up with shopping bags. I said, 'Excuse me, Madam, but what do you think of Murray Mints?' She put her bags down, pondered for a moment and then replied, 'Ah, they're very good – they bring the wind up at both ends!'

-.-.-.-

One of my favourite venues, where I appeared many times, was the Cresta Club in Solihull. I was booked for a week there with Diana Dors. We both had the same management so it was one of many such engagements for a while. The week went well until the Saturday night. She had an earlier booking at a hotel and things ran extremely late. I was just gearing up to do an impossible third lengthy spot when she eventually arrived. Talk about heart stopping!

-.-.-.-

My only time at the London Palladium was a one-nighter, in 1974, in a bill that included Matt Monro, Max Wall and Tommy Trinder and played to two packed houses. The impresario responsible, some months later, due to other financial pressures, committed suicide by jumping out of a hotel window. My personal sorrow is that I never met him to say 'Thank you' for a precious experience at the most famous theatre in the world.

CATERING FOR ALL

The local transport café is known, throughout the area, for the quality of its cuisine. The Health Inspector has just opened an office in there.

It's so low grade even the mice eat out.

Someone told me that they employ the only cook I have ever heard of who can burn salad.

Do not ask for a glass of water, under any circumstances - he can ruin that too.

The owner did contemplate going up-market but he abandoned the idea when it meant buying a dishwasher.

Fortunately, just down the road, a high-class restaurant opened last Xmas with a sign that read, 'Have your office party with us – you won't live to regret it.'

The chef came direct from an important position at the Café de Paris. He was their Maintenance Man.

The Maître d' keeps a disciplined regime – it's probably the whip that does it.

I don't think their pay system is up to scratch. Apparently, the waiters think the tips are wages.

I only went there once. Expensive – I couldn't afford to look at the menu!

The menu is in French. I took a chance, tried to remember my school lessons and finished up ordering the manager.

My friend took a girl there to try and create a good impression. When he went to pay the bill, his credit card dissolved.

SIGN UP

On my travels, as a musician and as a comedian, signs were always a source of merriment. Fortunately, all my life I have always carried a pen, a notebook and/or a lively imagination.

On a café wall: 'Too many cooks spoil the broth. Here we can make do with one.'

On a garden wall: 'Beware of the dog. (The cat is not over-friendly either.)'

In America: The Reliable Shoe Shop was renamed 'Acme Shoes - formerly Reliable.'

In a tailor's: 'Trust the customer. Beware of the bank.'

On a tailor's window: 'Come in here and have a fit.'

In a cinema favoured by young couples: 'Come early and get a back seat.'

On a club wall: 'Gentlemen must wear a tie. Other items of clothing are optional.'

In a corner shop: 'Please do not ask for credit, because it only upsets the wife.'

Outside a chemist's shop: 'Only prescribed drugs supplied.' Underneath, in chalk, 'For all others, see Nobby.'

In a hospital, after a spate of thefts: 'If you find anything missing, have a word with our security staff.'

In an eel and pie shop: 'If something slithers past you, it's probably the owner.'

A notice in a dentist's waiting room: 'Painless dental treatment.' Underneath in handwriting, 'The dentist won't feel a thing.'

Passing through a restaurant kitchen, on the way to what purported to be a dressing room, I saw, 'Don't dish the dirt.'

On the side of a garage: 'Our repairs won't dent your wallet.'

In a dressing room: 'Make sure that the Entertainment Secretary pays you in a good light.'

Dressing rooms were always a place to find scribbled messages – here is one from a comic: 'Elsewhere they bury their dead.'

And it was possibly the same one who had written on a girl singer's photo, 'If she sings like she looks – buyer beware.'

The North East was always considered the most difficult area for any of us involved in the business of invoking laughter. I once saw a road sign telling me 'To Newcastle.' Somebody had chalked under it, 'Known as "The Comic's Graveyard".'

Sunderland to me was the most difficult city. There was some advice on the wall in the digs: 'I came, I saw, I failed to conquer.'

I was tempted to add to that, 'My sympathy, whoever you are, I shared all of that with you.'

Outside a church: 'The End Is Nigh.' Next to it was a board listing all the events for the next 12 months.

And, would you believe, 'Love is all around you.' Next to it was an official notice, 'Beware of pickpockets.'

MAKING A MARK

An elderly lady named Rose
Had designs on a man and it shows.
It's not what you think,
When they'd both had a drink,
She'd tattooed him from shoulder to toes.

SOMETHING IN THE AIR

A beauty consultant from Maine
Bought a perfume to drive men insane.
But I'm sad to report
That some of them thought
The problem was one with the drain.

STRICTLY FOR PLEASURE

There was a young girl from Tyrone
Did nothing all day except moan.
'If it's not face to face,
As is often the case,
I do the best that I can on the phone.'

THE KNACK

A would-be chef known as Young Gretel
Was the worst in her college at Settle.
'I can't bake or cook
But you'll find, if you look'
I'm a dab hand at filling a kettle.'

DIGGING IN AGAIN

Back to the digs again for that endless source of amusement, the comments from the clubland acts, as they returned from triumph or, more often, it seems, disaster.

'He said you weren't the worst act they'd had at the club but you came a close second.'

-.-.-.-

'Don't be put off by the look of the place. When you arrive, even the car park looks unfriendly.'

-.-.-.-

'I won't say they are all on the fiddle there but I had to bribe the bloke on the door to get in.'

-.-.-.-

'The comedian was so filthy last night, I noticed even the committee were laughing.'

-.-.-.-

'He said to me, "Don't sing any songs from that musical, *Fiddler on the Roof*. They don't like religious songs here." '

-.-.-.-

'That's got to be the smallest club the group has ever played in. Our drummer and the Entertainment Secretary had to share a stool.'

-.-.-.-

'He seemed okay though. He asked me to turn the volume up a bit as he could still hear the Steward shouting at the members.'

ACT AS IF YOU CAN

When I decided to become an actor one of my first jobs was as an extra in the film *I'm All Right Jack*. In the big crowd scene, I'm the 14th dissenter from the right.

As soon as I told our Amdram company I was applying to join RADA they signed me up for RADAR– so they would know I was coming.

I'd just finished playing the lead part in their pantomime *Puss in Boots*. My God, it's hot in that cat costume.

The next production will be George Bernard Shaw's *Arms and the Man*. I thought I'd give them a hand.

Acting is easy really. All you have to do is to learn a few lines and try not to nod off when somebody else has a long bit.

My tip is - don't bother learning the whole play. Just learn your part and then when everyone stops talking and turns to you, you'll know it's your line.

Anyway, I did the RADA audition. I haven't heard from them yet but I think they liked me. I heard one of the women say I ought to get a job as a stage hand.

I even auditioned for radio drama but I got the impression that my face didn't fit.

How many actors does it take to change a light bulb? It can't happen – they wouldn't make an entrance without decent illumination.

Acting is the silliest profession you could imagine. You pretend to be other people, you change your voice and accent, you wear daft clothes and you play out ridiculous stories. It's absolutely a childish fantasy world – and you can see why so many of us love it.

MOTOR WAYS

The police are investigating a number of petrol station robberies. Apparently, the thief demands that the victim hands over every penny they possess. Officers are anxious to interview the Chancellor of the Exchequer.

An animal escaped from London Zoo and several people on the M1 reckoned that they saw a zebra crossing.

A Birds Eye van containing an assortment of custard, jelly and blancmange was in a collision with a vehicle carrying cake mix earlier today. The police said it was just a trifle.

The number of road traffic accidents on the M6 has dramatically reduced since the introduction of speed bumps.

Heavy flooding on the motorway has seen the highway patrols being replaced by The Royal Lifeboat Service.

Due to expenditure cutbacks on all UK motorways, in future, all breakdowns will be repaired by Burton's Quick Fix of Caterham.

Police were called to a service station after a fight broke out between a group of football referees. A whistle was blown and the referees awarded everyone a penalty.

The service station has been closed down until further notice, after it was discovered that the notice 'Buy one, get one free' actually referred to the female staff.

A section of the M1 had to be closed after a lorry transporting preserves overturned, causing what was described by some of the onlookers as a very nasty jam.

In future, there will be no more jokes allowed involving the motorways, after the Minister for Transport had a very severe breakdown.

MY FEUD WITH FREUD

I had problems with Sir Clement Freud (politician, broadcaster, writer and chef). In his pre-knight days, he was a panellist on ATV's *New Faces* and I the warm-up comic. I walked into the studio to find him already seated reading a newspaper. I asked him politely if he could lower the paper while I did my bit. He totally ignored me. I struggled on with the audience fascinated by this man behaving badly and so I whispered, 'Please put the paper down.' Nothing. So I barked like a sergeant major, 'Lower the paper!' The newspaper shot down and he stared ahead for the rest of my spot, like a man transfixed. Next week, in his newspaper column, he fired back. It read, in effect, '- the comedian came on, cracked a few unfunny jokes and nobody laughed.' Round 2 to Clement – but don't leave, there is more to come.

A few months later, I compèred a cabaret show in Kenilworth. Guess who had decided to become a comic? My act and the girl singer's were well received but then came his top of the bill time. Well, I've seen some disasters but nothing like this. The problem was he was a mumbler. Couple that with no mic technique and you've got the picture. After five minutes, management decided something had to be done and a stagehand crept along in the dark, pushing the mic stand towards our star (often nothing is more noticeable than someone who doesn't want to be seen). Out of the corner of his eye, he saw the mic advancing and he started retreating. The farce ended with our featured player standing at the back of the stage, beautifully lit but still inaudible. After an interminable period, he muttered something that I guessed was his act's end. I came on, trying to raise some applause. As we walked along the corridor, he muttered, 'I don't know why they booked you tonight.' I'd had enough of him and couldn't resist, 'I think they thought someone ought to get some laughs.'

(For those of you who haven't seen this excerpt from *Laughs In The Right Place,* I thought you might enjoy this, courtesy of Brewin Books Ltd)

COURT IN TIME

My brother was up before the Beak last year. He tried to tell people he'd been to the Parrot House at the London Zoo.

The charge sheet, when it was read out in the court, would have embarrassed Al Capone.

The officer who gave evidence said he thought bro was trying to join up all the dots.

The Judge, in his summary, remarked that they had come into contact so often he would like to invite him to the Magistrates' Christmas Party.

He accepted on condition that he did not have to dance with the Judge this time.

The Prison Governor welcomed him back and said he hoped he didn't mind being on his own in solitary confinement.

It is his favourite gaol, though. The last time he was there, he tried to have them included in the Michelin Good Food Guide.

My brother and his wife don't exactly get on. He's one of the few prisoners on record to apply for late release.

What do they call a privately-owned phone in a prison? A cell phone.

How many prison warders does it take to change a light bulb? They would never do it. They'd spend too much time, busy arguing over how it got out.

'Have you ever been up before me?'
'I don't know, Your Honour, what time do you get up?'

WEATHER RETORTS

Due to global warming, this year Father Xmas will be arriving by kayak pulled by six dolphins.

Noddy Holder will be abandoning his customary festive song and recording *The Sun Has Got His Hat On.*

Following extremely strong winds in the north, Grimsby and Liverpool are now joined at the hip and will, in future, be known as Grimlin.

In the south, London can be found floating six miles out from the east coast.

The dense fog resulted in milkmen all over the country delivering to the wrong addresses. Several housewives claimed they are very satisfied with their new best friends.

Heavy flooding occurred in the Birmingham City versus Aston Villa match yesterday. The referee is now listed in the *Guinness Book of Records* for covering the most swimming laps in a football match.

The heatwave in the Westminster region has been blamed on the hot air emanating from the House of Commons during Prime Minister's Question Time.

Following several months of unprecedented snowfalls, the Abominable Snowman has been elected Mayor of Halifax.

It has not rained in Manchester for almost ten minutes – the council have issued a drought warning.

Personally, I had decided not to go fishing with my brother today, due to weather reports of very inclement weather. He has just been brought home suffering with severe sunburn.

The man in charge of the weather programme on our local television channel must be using a cracked crystal ball.

Listening to older people talking about the difficulties of getting to and from school in the winter of 1946, I'm amazed that they have managed to get home yet.

I remember Grandma saying that, when Grandpa arrived home from work, she had to thaw him out with three hot water bottles and the friendly woman from next door.

I've never believed her story that the knock on the door was the kids' snowman, pleading to come in for a warm.

The October issue of the *Bexhill Clarion* says that, after the diabolical summer, the council are delighted to announce, for the first time, the complete absence of visitors.

Heavy sudden snow in Heckmondwike has completely covered the area and four elderly ladies waiting for a bus.

News of a volcanic eruption in Doncaster this morning may have been slightly exaggerated.

All talk of global warming has been discarded since it was discovered that camels in the Sahara are now being fitted with snow boots.

There have been so many complaints about recent weather forecasts that all applicants for the job have to take a lie detector test.

In Karachi, the Test Match was held up for a few minutes to allow the snow plough to completely clear the pitch.

It gave the physio time to treat the England wicketkeeper for snow blindness.

So far, newspaper reports concerning the appearance of a snow-covered yeti have not yet been confirmed.

The tornado that swept through Port Talbot was responsible for the disappearance of quite a few chimneys and Mrs Gwyneth Hughes of Lower Valley Road, who was last seen flying in the direction of Pontrhydyfen.

I am not going to France again on holiday until I get a written assurance that the weather will be fine.

STRANGE, ISN'T IT?

I think I'll always stay at home
A rabbit in its warren,
Each time I go abroad I find
Everyone else is foreign!

THE UNEXPECTED SIDE OF SHOWBIZ

Neville Brand: The gravelly-voiced character actor, the veteran of dozens of American films and TV dramas. He was reputed to be the 4th most decorated soldier in the Second World War, something he frequently denied. Despite his tough image, he was a bibliophile with a collection of over 30,000 books.

-.-.-.-

Christopher Lee: Famous mainly for his horror roles, he was also the possessor of a magnificent singing voice. He not only recorded several operas and musicals but also took part in *Charlemagne by the Sword and Cross,* the symphonic heavy metal album, in his late 90s.

-.-.-.-

The Sons of Lee Marvin: It was a humorous secret society created in his name. In order to be a member, you had to have some family resemblance. The only person to complain was one of his sons.

-.-.-.-

Christopher Walken: Before breaking into films, he was an assistant lion tamer in a circus.

-.-.-.-

Ronald Reagan: The 40th President of America, in 1960, failed an audition for a part in the play *The Best Man.* The producer decided that he did not look enough like a President.

-.-.-.-

Helen Mirren: Her father, Vasily Petrovich Mironoff, was a member of the exiled Russian aristocracy.

-.-.-.-

Jack Nicholson: The American actor, in his late 30s, discovered that his mother was, in reality, his sister.

7934 Sinatra: This was an asteroid named after the singer Frank Sinatra.

-.-.-.-

Elton John: He is purported to use pseudonyms when booking into hotels, such as Lillian Lollipop and Sir Humphrey Handbag.

-.-.-.-

John Inman: I worked with him on the long-running TV series *Are You Being Served* but it wasn't until we met up again at Beacon Radio, in Wolverhampton, that he told me that he had had plenty of practice for his role as Mr Humphreys. When he left school, he worked at two gentlemen's outfitters, including a stint at Austin Reed's in Regent Street, in the heart of London.

-.-.-.-

Harry H. Corbett: Famous as the rag-and-bone man in *Steptoe and Son* he served in the Far East in 1945, deserted and then handed himself in to the Military Police. Punishment unknown. According to an actor friend of his, he was also an accomplished juggler.

-.-.-.-

Edwin Richfield: I recorded quite a few BBC radio plays with him. He was also one of the stars of the TV series *Interpol*. He had rather a stern visage but that hid an enormous sense of fun. He and his wife had a home brew shop, in Shrewsbury.

-.-.-.-

Bob Monkhouse: I was the warm-up comedian for ATV's *The Golden Shot* and he was one of the most brilliant minds I have ever met. In 2007, he posthumously appeared in an advertisement promoting awareness of prostate cancer.

Bernard Manning: The comic was often severely criticised for his racist jokes, but there was another side to him. He named his house 'Shalom', which is the Hebrew word for 'Peace'. His next-door neighbour was an Asian doctor who said he was the kindest person he had ever known. He was also constantly taking part in concerts promoted by any number of religious charities. I found him to be very good company, as long as you were prepared for a verbal jousting.

THE ACTOR'S LAMENT

My 10 x 8's arrived today
But apart from looking old and bored
All that's missing underneath
Is a warning note and a large reward.

THE SHOPPING EXPERIENCE

When I heard he was opening it as a corner shop, I was quite disappointed that he didn't actually sell corners.

It was a bit ominous when the opening ceremony was performed by a bailiff.

The advert in his window on the first day produced a few interesting responses: 'Female assistant required – must be experienced.'

His advertising slogans also received a mixed reception:

> 'Our service is second to one.'
>
> 'For our opening hours please try the door.'
>
> 'Stealing does not count as self-service checkout.'
>
> 'You will not be overcharged for inferior goods.'
>
> 'Our online shopping will continue as soon as I've repaired the puncture.'

Over all, the shop has been a success – some customers have been there twice.

'Could you put my milk in the bag, please?'
'No, Madam, it comes in cartons.'

'I want some of that stuff that isn't butter and it isn't margarine.'
'How about a pound of lard?'

'Madam, how long do you want this roll of tape?'
'Well, actually, I was hoping to be able to keep it.'

HAVING RELATIONS

DAD

He was known as an odd job man. It wasn't so much the jobs that were odd.

A very level headed person – which made wearing a bowler hat almost impossible.

His motto was 'If ever I can give you a hand.' Where he got the spare parts from was his business.

Dad had problems getting a licence to marry Mum. The prison authorities had to grant one.

I am not sure if it was a happy marriage or not but Mum applied for a divorce in the Registry Office.

They made a conscious decision not the have children. My sister and I were teenagers at the time.

Dad supported Aston Villa and Birmingham City football teams and regularly wore their scarves simultaneously with pride. When they played each other, he got beaten up by both sets of fans.

By coincidence, his birth date was the same as King Charles III. He said they decided not to send each other birthday cards.

He started work as a bus conductor in 1995. No one liked to tell him they hadn't employed any for years.

Then he tried to get a job as a sheepherder but there wasn't much demand for that in Croydon.

After that, he lived off the fat of the land for years. Mum hated being called that.

MUM

The family were so poor when I was born the stork cancelled the delivery charge.

She took one look at me and tried to contact the Returns Department.

Later on, waiting at the school gates, she told the other mothers she was only doing it for a dare.

Cooking was never her strong point – she had to consult an instruction booklet to manage toast.

In fact, her cooking was so bad Dad had a water sprinkler fitted and Mum swapped her apron for a set of oilskins.

She was a strict mother though. When she heard that one of the MPs had had the whip removed she asked if she could borrow it.

My parents had so many fights they sold the lounge suite and bought a row of ringside seats.

I remember once she asked Dad if she could go to a Health Farm to recover. He booked her for a fortnight as a muck spreader.

She was one of twins. So was her sibling.

They were often mistaken for one another – I think it was the beard.

She couldn't be described as a literate woman. Her lengthiest word was 'Don't'.

I suppose, on reflection, she wasn't such a bad mother and she gave me food for thought – which was preferable to her cooking.

SIBLINGS

My brother and I had so many disputes the Arbitration Board issued us with season tickets.

We are twins – I deny identical – but he keeps insisting that he is the elder. I think he was born with a stopwatch in his hand.

He should have gone into Showbiz as an impressionist – he drinks like a fish and the resemblance doesn't end there.

I call him Moses because every time he opens his mouth, the bull rushes.

He applied to be an apprentice to Father Xmas. I'm sure it was the holidays that appealed to him.

He's just bought himself a house built entirely of glass – well, not entirely - it's got brick windows.

Sister is a keen golfer but, being on the small side she thinks the holes are bunkers.

She's married to a burglar and last night, she heard a noise, woke him and said, 'I think we've got a policeman downstairs.'

Their house is right on the edge of a river. They would leave but she says the damp is good for her bamboo shoots.

And they keep having children! I went in to the kids' bedroom and it's the first time I've seen wall-to-wall feet.

Their major problem is that they are both drinkers. Last week the brewery next door complained about the fumes.

ME AND ROLF

Rolf Harris and his descent from fame into notoriety are well documented elsewhere but I thought you might like to hear about my dealings with him.

One Sunday, in the early 70s, Rolf Harris was the Golden Partner on *The Golden Shot*. This very talented Australian entertainer was then at the top of his popularity. Along with many others, I was looking forward to meeting him.

I always arrived early to watch rehearsals and help the guests in any way. When I saw a screen being erected, I thought it best to have a word with him. I said, 'Rolf, I'm the warm-up comic and I wondered if I could help. I see you are singing a duet with yourself so do you want me to explain to the audience that your image will also be on film?' He angrily barked at me, 'Film? Film? It's video, you fool!' I was taken aback, 'I realise that but hardly any of the audience will have video recorders yet and most will not know what video is. I don't think it's patronising to refer to it as "film".' He was furious. 'You mention "film" and I'll come out on the floor and tell the audience that the warm-up comic is an idiot.' I shook my head, 'Okay, I'll say nothing.' So, I didn't. The result was that the audience looked bewildered, not knowing whether to watch him or the screen. I am quite convinced it halved the impact of his spot. I derived no satisfaction from knowing he got his comeuppance because my sole intention with every programme, was to help ensure its success.

However, the saga doesn't end there. Shortly afterwards I noticed one of the make-up girls standing to one side, looking very upset. I asked her what was wrong. She replied, 'All the girls are having an argument about who does Rolf Harris's make-up.' I said, 'I didn't know he was that popular.' She stared back at me, 'It's not that he's popular – it's like dealing with a f------ octopus!'

Subsequent courtroom revelations showed we were far from being the only ones with problems with Mr Harris.

TAKING A BREAK

My neighbour has just come back from Tenerife. I couldn't even afford to go to Ninerife.

The only time I ever went to Spain was under a pseudonym and a heavy black beard.

That's exactly how we got caught. My wife decided to do exactly the same thing

Mind you, she's never been big on holidays. Actually, that's not true – she's big everywhere.

When she lies on the beach, they have to ask her to move to let the tide in.

I wouldn't like to intimate that she takes a lot of clothes on holiday but a week in Weston-Super-Mare necessitates hiring a large team of native bearers.

It's not fair, is it? She moans if I take two handkerchiefs.

She complained bitterly to the council about the violence on the beach but they told her that traditionally they have always had a Punch and Judy Man.

First day, at the hotel, she summoned the Manager to tell him that the soup was cold. He explained that Chilled Spring Pea Soup is always served cold.

He then went on to ask her if we were on honeymoon. His family says, with a bit of luck, they should be able to visit him, in hospital, sometime next week.

NOT JUST PRETENCE

Quite a few well-known actors 'got their knees brown' (military parlance for being in the Forces) during WWII.

Richard Todd: Became an Army Captain and participated in the D Day landings and the capture of Pegasus Bridge. He later played Major Howard in the film *A Bridge Too Far.*

-.-.-.-

Michael Caine: Called up for National Service, he served in Germany and Korea. In 1956, he appeared in *A Hill in Korea.*

-.-.-.-

Jon Pertwee: Was in the Royal Navy for six years, later joining Naval Intelligence. For seventeen years he played a Chief Petty Officer in the BBC radio programme *The Navy Lark.*

-.-.-.-

David Niven: Took part in the invasion of Norway and rose to the rank of Lieutenant-Colonel. At one time, he was Glenn Miller's boss.

-.-.-.-

Alec Guinness: Commanded a landing craft in the invasion of Italy.

-.-.-.-

James Stewart: Joined up in 1943, flying on bombing missions in Germany and Nazi-occupied France. After the war, he stayed in the Air Force Reserve and became a Brigadier General.

-.-.-.-

Clark Gable: At the age of 43, he joined the US Army Air Force and flew five combat missions as an observer-gunner.

TROUBLE IN PARADISE

Every so often, the unexpected occurs that no one could make allowances for. These incidents, strangely, all involve some of the nicest people you could ever meet!

In May 1980 Bill Owen, the star of the TV series *Last of the Summer Wine,* was a guest on the BBC's *Saturday Night at the Mill.* To the audiences' surprise, he appeared in evening dress with his hair slicked back – looking as unlike his character Compo as could be imagined.

-.-.-.-

The same year, the BBC decided to reduce the number of orchestras they used. The musicians naturally staged a protest. On one of the coldest days of the year I saw the most heart-breaking sight. That superb pianist/organist, Harold Rich, was sitting outside Pebble Mill, in Birmingham, shivering in the cold. I have often wondered what effect that had on those precious hands.

-.-.-.-

In 1982 author and politician Norman St John Stevas was invited to be interviewed on *Pebble Mill at One* about his new book *Pope John Paul II; His Travels and Mission.* Unfortunately, part way through the interview, the book's jacket slipped to reveal a different book underneath. His own copy, I was told, had not arrived in time for the programme.

-.-.-.-

Comedian Stan Stennett, one of the most easy-going, likeable characters I have ever met, was a guest on ATV's *The Golden Shot.* The Director, Dicky Leaman, checked with him about his gags and Stan said he was going to accompany himself on guitar and sing *Pennies From Heaven.* Dicky insisted on jokes but was told that Stan did not have enough time, at such short notice, to prepare a spot. Dicky and Director, Les Cocks, were very disgruntled and poor Stan was extremely upset.

MORE TREASURES FROM MY PAST

As I mentioned, in *I Look At It Like This*, the Jewish Social Club in Moseley, where my band had a Sunday residency for two years, was a fount of good gags:

I've got to be up early in the morning. I'm playing the lead in the new Jewish James Bond film *Moishe Bond is Oy-Oy-7.*

She changed her name from 'Carmen' to 'Cohen' and then back to 'Cohen' from 'Carmen' and then back again to ---- honestly, that girl doesn't know if she's 'Carmen' or 'Cohen'.

Our rabbi has got ideas above his station. He's insisting on wearing a fur-lined yarmulke.

I told them about a friend of mine, at a bar mitzvah we played at, who always tells me that his far-fetched stories are true. He said, 'Only this morning, my brother came round to our house, pleading to borrow some money. I asked him, "Aren't you ashamed begging like this?" He shook his head, "I'm not begging at all. It's just a transfer of finances within the family" '

He reckoned he told his brother one day, 'Help you out? Help you out? I've got nothing and next to nothing of that!'

My wife insists I'm always telling lies. I asked her how she could possibly know. She said, 'Your lips are still moving.'

One member claimed he and his wife were always arguing. We asked him why he married her. He said, 'Because she wouldn't say "No". 'She wouldn't say "No"?' "That's right. I asked her to marry me and she wouldn't say, "No."

I remember, one Sunday, during the interval, I told a joke and everybody laughed but one man. He just sat there, looking thoughtful. I said to him, 'That's a sure way of killing a joke – trying to analyse it.' He said, 'That's my job – I'm an analyst.' And he was!

JUST A FEW ODD 'UNS

I spent a whole summer season with a fellow comedian who was under the impression that his wife was a total spendthrift. Every other day, he would tear a pound note in half and post it to her. The following day, he would send the other half. I have often wondered how much she must have spent, each year, on rolls of Sellotape!

-.-.-.-

Ken Windsor, my friend, met Brian Wilde in the street and told him how much he enjoyed his portrayal of Foggy Dewhurst in *Last of the Summer Wine*. He said, 'What do you think of the character?' Brian replied, 'He's a very silly man!'

(I must be a bit dense because I always wondered why he was called 'Foggy'. It suddenly hit me – it probably comes from the old traditional Irish song, 'The Foggy Dew')

-.-.-.-

Seeking to extend my journalistic activities, in the late 70s, I rang our local paper, the *Northfield Messenger*, and told the Editor that, as there were so many acts living in the area, a regular fortnightly column could prove quite popular. He agreed but prophesied it would only last a couple of months. It lasted for a couple of years!

One of the people I got in touch with was the manager of a girl singer. I asked him if he could let me have a photograph and a brief rundown of her career. He thought for a moment and then said, 'No, I don't think I'll bother. If it had been for the *Daily Mirror* or one of the other nationals, I might have taken the trouble – but as it's only for a local paper, I can't waste the time.' I said, 'Oh, I am sorry to have troubled you. I wouldn't have needed to ask for info or a picture if we had been talking about Shirley Bassey but as it's only ...'

HEREABOUTS

Parents have written to the council about the inadequate heating at the infants' school. From next month, the new radiators, outside the school railings, will be switched on 30 minutes prior to departure times.

Some confusion has arisen since the manager of the furniture shop on The Parade announced that it will be closing *tout suite.*

A team of volunteers has expressed the hope that 'By the end of the week, we will have completed the clearance of the area and Miss Edna Mayberry at No 27.'

The Electric Car Showroom on The Parade has had its extension refused.

Rowdyism, violence, drugs and the repeated use of extremely bad language has resulted in the closure of the Evensong Senior Citizens' Club.

Due to the strong winds on Monday, the paper shop in Green Lane has blown away.

The new shoe repairer, on the corner of Green Street, has withdrawn his complaint to the police, after it was explained to him that no offence was intended by older residents with their frequent repetition of the word 'Cobblers'.

As residents will be aware, the traffic lights on the High Street have been permanently fixed on stop. One elderly person said it took him four days to get back from the local shops.

Following the receipt of an email from Mr Liversidge, re the blockage at the end of his road, the Highways Department have reminded him that he lives in a cul-de-sac.

SHOWBIZ MISCELLANY No 2

From the department of 'You-can't-win-'em-all'. Halfway through my act at Boston Cabaret Club, three Chinamen suddenly appeared, in the doorway. Like a good comic, I couldn't resist it. 'There you are, folks, people travel from all over the world to see my act!' Cue big laugh. Afterwards, the owner was absolutely furious. 'You ridiculed a group of my biggest gamblers!' Ah, well.

-.-.-.-

Arriving at RAF Scampton, I found it was the annual contest between officers and sergeants. In every room, the two teams were competing at darts, snooker, bowls-along-the-corridor, and even unarmed combat. Nothing they did, however, could upstage the previous year's events. The new Station Commander had arrived on the very day of the competition. His first attempt at socialising was to take part in the five-a-side football match in the main mess hall. Within two hours, they had to carry him out on a stretcher, with a broken leg! So, when I opened my act with, 'Well, if you don't find my spot funny, the Group Captain has offered to break his leg again!' you can imagine the reaction!

-.-.-.-

I was the warm-up comedian for all of Norman Vaughan's time as compère of ATV's *The Golden Shot*. One afternoon, wearing his microphone, Norman, not knowing it was already switched on, had to make an emergency trip to the loo. The audience were treated to the sound of Niagara Falls.

-.-.-.-

One afternoon, a small case was discovered on the edge of the *Golden Shot* set. A group of security men gathered some distance away. I heard mutterings, 'Terrorists!', 'I knew this would happen! 'etc. When they got to the point where the bomb squad were about to be called, the piano tuner walked round the corner, picked up his case and with a cheery, 'See you next week,' he was off.

WORKMATES

Over the years, I worked with all three of bandleader Ted Heath's best-known singers, Dickie Valentine, Dennis Lotis and Lita Roza. By coincidence, Dickie came to my mother's for tea and Dennis took me to meet his mum on holiday here from S Africa. The trilogy is incomplete as there are no maternal memories of Lita and me.

-.-.-.-

One of the most unusual comedy acts was that of Johnnie 'Goon' Tweed. The more astute of you will gather his whole act was based on *The Goon Show* radio programmes. I spent a very enjoyable week with this highly intelligent man when we were both part of The Peddlers show at Allinson's in Litherland, but it wasn't until the end of our time together that I discovered that, in the daytime, he worked at a hotel in Manchester, and was a Cordon Bleu chef.

-.-.-.-

I got on extremely well with Bob Monkhouse and Norman Vaughan while I was the warm-up comic on *The Golden Shot* but Charlie Williams and I never hit it off. After I compèred the show in 1974, due to Norman's illness, a local newspaper campaigned to get me the job permanently – not at my instigation, I hasten to add. Someone told Charlie and for six months, he walked around me like a man walking on eggshells.

-.-.-.-

The brilliant Scottish accordionist Lawrie Adam and I did a summer season together at the Knightstone Theatre in Weston-super-Mare in 1970, in *Summer Showboat* with Tony Mercer. We not only shared a dressing room but a lot of laughter. We followed this with pantomime in Hastings at the White Rock Pavilion, in *Puss in Boots*. Some years later, I was flabbergasted to discover that Lawrie had become a vicar and a video co-ordinator at the Church of England, with his own regular religious television programme.

March 1979 found me at La Reserve, the Midland restaurant, set in the heart of Sutton Park – top of the bill was Welsh singer, Ivor Emmanuel. Not only was he a very fine singer but he had also appeared in *Zulu*. He told me a lovely story about an incident in the filming. The Zulus were advancing and his character thought it a good idea to counter their chanting by singing *Men of Harlech*. He sang but they kept coming. Desperately, he and the other Welsh sang louder and louder but still they kept surging forward. The first bare foot had just touched the stockade when Ivor's Cockney pal whispered to him, 'I think you'd better sing 'em something they know, Taffy!'

-.-.-.-

I appeared in over forty shows with Paul Daniels and one afternoon, in Lowestoft, he insisted on treating Jo and me to a cream tea. Jumping into the back of the car, his diminutive figure was immediately smothered by our Old English Sheepdog, Groucho (who was as fond of Paul as we were). I said, 'Oh, I'm so sorry!' From under a mound of fur, a muffled voice replied, 'No, please don't – I think I'm in love!'

-.-.-.-

Irish singer Ruby Murray was another nice artiste. Sadly, on one Bristol show, they booked her with the by-then better-known Irish singer, Dana. We tried to console Ruby but she was heartbroken. No wonder she needed a drink.

-.-.-.-

I did a handful of theatre shows with Peters and Lee. At The Forum, in Barrow-in-Furness, Lennie who, despite being blind, was a notorious practical joker, decided between shows that it was time for a jape. He stuffed a piece of paper in the water key of my trombone. The result was that I couldn't produce a note. The end of my act was ruined, the audience was completely mystified, the band was totally embarrassed and the only one amused was Lennie Peters.

Kenny Baker was a Brummie lad from Sheldon. He became well known for his role as R2-D2 in *Star Wars.* but I worked with him when he was one half of the Minitones and also when he was the resident compère at Cleopatra's, in Easter Compton. Sometime later, he introduced me to his family in London – although he and his wife had dwarfism, both their sons were of normal height.

-.-.-.-

Trevor Bannister played the golf captain, Toby Mulberry Smith, in *Last of the Summer Wine* and we met when I was 'warming-up' the sit-com, *Are You Being Served.* He was shortly due to start a summer season in a farce at Weymouth Pavilion. When I told him that I would be there for some Sunday concerts with Tony Mercer he promised that I would have the regular use of his dressing room. He was as good as his word.

-.-.-.-

One *Golden Shot* afternoon, Johnnie Hamp, the distinguished TV producer and the brains behind the hugely successful series *The Comedians,* was one of the guests. Later on, he said how much he had enjoyed my warm-up and suggested that, at some point, I should give him a ring. I never did and, to this day, regret that, not because I might have missed out on something like *The Comedians* (for which, in my opinion, I would have been completely unsuitable) but simply because I have always admired his work.

I am very grateful that, through Facebook, we have been friends for quite a while now.

FIT FOR PURPOSE

Fitness is all in the mind, and that's the best excuse I can come up with for not exercising.

I've finally joined a gym but I don't really have to believe it if I don't want to.

The first day, there was a bit of a scramble, due to lack of equipment. I went on the rowing machine but all the other members were in the same boat.

Not much activity today, so the instructor offered to sew some sequins on my track suit.

My wife only joined because she misread the notice. She thought it said, 'Keep fat'.

Today she was wearing a leotard. She asked, 'How do you think my figure looks in this?' I said, 'Advancing or retreating?'

I'm just about fit for football again. It must be years since I watched the Albion.

Australia has asked the Olympics to include boomerang throwing next year but, so far, there has been no comeback.

My brother is a bit on the small side. When he plays golf, his warning shout is, 'Two!'

I tried boxing. My first fight I was weaving and bobbing, weaving and bobbing. I didn't win but I finished three baskets and a Persian rug.

I was on the canvas so often they called me 'Rembrandt'.

I've been told that jogging is good for the system - tell somebody holding a pint that, when you jog their elbow!

And running - does that count racing your pigeons?

My family thought nothing of going to a fitness club. In fact, I don't imagine they ever thought of it at all.

Dad tried a set of chest expanders, let go of one end and finished up in Edinburgh.

The gym included me in the Sports Day presentations. They decided I was just about fit enough to hold the owner's coat.

They entered me in the Over 80s 100 yard sprint. I wouldn't mind but I don't qualify for another 37 years.

Next year, I intend to go in for a Marathon. You know, those stewards who hand out the water.

The other night, I dreamed I was swimming in the freezing English Channel. When I woke up, my feet were in the fridge and my head in the dog's bowl.

In the Highland Games, one High Jump athlete insisted on competing in a strong wind, wearing a kilt. He was disqualified for making a parachute landing. (Several elderly ladies had to be treated for shock.)

Critics of the caber champion's performance called him a 'Tosser' without realising he was supposed to be!

I tried squatting at the gym but the police made me move on.

How many tennis players does it take to change a light bulb? None, they would never accept it was out.

They suggested using a stopwatch on me at the gym. I said they'd be better using a sundial.

Why did they think the footballer was seeing things? Because he said two of the rooms were changing.

QUICK FIT

As quick as a spear
Thrown by the Masai,
As quick as a fading
Glint from a glass eye,
As quick as you can say
'Cucumber',
As quick as you can
Think of a number,
As quick as I
Can misspell 'gnu',
That's as quick as it took
To fall for you.

TIMED OUT

Just as time
Killed the horse and carriage
Romance was killed
By the thought of marriage.

LAUGH LINES

Marriages that seek
To find perfection
Waste some time
In introspection.
Spend that time
(At least a half)
By trying to make
Each other laugh.

FURTHER RAMBLINGS

You might like to see another 1979 newspaper column:

THE WEEK A STRIPPER STRIPPED MY KITCHEN

With a male stripper stripping the kitchen and a singing compère flitting around the bedrooms, it's been quite a week! We've finally fought our way into our new house. With help from Andy Wade, that be-whiskered, muscles-running-to-fat comedian-stripper tearing paper off kitchen walls, and singing compère Tony Greene from La Reserve helping, we've achieved the almost impossible – decorating, painting and moving all in one week.

Groucho, my Old English sheepdog, can't believe his luck with a real garden to race around. We've been very happy in our little community in Dominic Drive which is why we're only two miles away, still in Kings Norton. We're nearer West Heath Hospital where for two consecutive years, Jo and I had the pleasure of opening their annual fête. I hope this year's event will be a huge success. I'm only sorry I will be working away that day.

Charity

Spring Bank Holiday found me in Northampton for the annual Haemophiliac charity cabaret – isn't it amazing how many worthwhile charities there are and how little we know about them? The next night, I was the sole 'turn' at a dinner for Legal and General Insurance Co at the Falcon Hotel, Stratford – just twenty top salesmen and yours truly, an ex-Britannic agent as their comedian!

On Saturday I met up again with one of Birmingham's top professional magic acts, Johnny Mysto and Juanita. Apart from having their own magic shop, these two tour the world, mystifying audiences with their own feats. At one point Johnny saws his better half in two halves – or was it three thirds? I couldn't believe my eyes, poor Juanita in a cabinet with their zig-zag effect really beggars description.

GETTING PERSONAL

You may be interested to see some of my favourite entertainment – if not, it should at least stimulate you to compile your own list:

FILMS

Westerns: *The Stalking Moon, Dances With Wolves, Unforgiven, Ride the High Country, The Naked Spur.* Most of Randolph Scott and Audie Murphy's westerns.

Political: *Darkest Hour, Gathering Storm, Frost Nixon.*

Musicals: *The Music Man, Fiddler On The Roof.*

Biographies: *The Glenn Miller Story, The Jolson Story, Jolson Sings Again.*

Thrillers: *The Ipcress File, The Day of the Jackal, Tinker Tailor Soldier Spy, Goodnight, and Good Luck.*

War: *The Train, A Bridge Too Far, Operation Amsterdam, Sea of Sand.*

Comedies: *Monsieur Hulot's Holiday, Play It Again Sam.*

Actors: Randolph Scott, James Stewart, Burt Lancaster, Gary Oldman,

Actresses: June Allyson, Judi Dench.

Comics: Jacques Tati, Laurel & Hardy.

TELEVISION

Drama: *Borgen, Wallander* (Swedish), *Endeavour, New Tricks.*

Comedies: *Last Of The Summer Wine, The Thin Blue Line. Andy Capp, The Worst Week of My Life.*

Actors: David Jason, Alan Armstrong, Krister Henriksson. Roger Allam

Actresses: Maxine Peake, Sidse Babett Knudsen.

Authors: Alan Bennett, Maureen Lipman, Ben Macintyre, Simon Hughes.

THE FILM GALLERY

A fellow we'll simply call Max
Collected photos in boxes and sacks.
I don't like them all
But they cover the wall
To hide all the dirt and the cracks.

TV HERE I COME

She arrived at the studio by car
Accompanied by her Pa and her Ma.
'I can't act, dance or sing,
I've no talent to bring
So I should be an overnight star.'

TRUE CONFESSION

June Allyson was my secret passion
When schoolboy crushes were the fashion.
American stars can change their name,
But, somehow, it doesn't feel the same,
To find to my complete surprise, man,
I was really in love with Eleanor Geisman.

Finally, some of my favourite quotations:

'If you had a face like mine, you'd punch me on the nose, and I'm just the man to do it.' (Stan Laurel)

'The louder he spoke of his honour, the faster we counted the spoons.' (Ralph Waldo Emerson)

'Whether you believe you can or you can't, you're right.' (Henry Ford)

'It is a good thing for an uneducated man to read books of quotations.' (Winston Churchill)

'Perhaps it is better to be irresponsible and right than to be responsible and wrong.' (Winston Churchill)

'You only live once, but if you do it right, once is enough.' (Mae West)

'I am willing to admit that I may not always be right, but I am never wrong.' (Samuel Goldwyn)

'Twenty years from now, you will be more disappointed by the things that you didn't do than by the ones you did do.' (Mark Twain)

'When I consider how my life is spent / I hardly ever repent.' (Ogden Nash)

'Whoever called it 'necking' was a poor judge of anatomy.' (Groucho Marx)

'In Italy for 30 years under the Borgias, they had warfare, terror, murder, bloodshed – they produced Michelangelo, Leonardo da Vinci and the Renaissance. In Switzerland, they had brotherly love, 500 years of democracy and peace and what did they produce--? The cuckoo clock!' (Orson Welles in *The Third Man.*)

THE CONTENTED MAN

I'll tell you now, it's late for me,
Of all the things I longed to be:
The driver of the fastest trains,
(I'd 'Toot, Toot, Toot' till the stoker complains.)

An explorer exploring Everest
So near the top I'd need a vest.
A doctor or a rural vet.
(The closest I got was the flu and a pet.)

To drink at least a yard of ale.
(One pint and I applied for bail.)
Will wonders of the world never cease?
I've almost finished *War and Peace.*

Audie Murphy, Randolph Scott,
Just two of the heroes I was not.
Ian Botham, centuries got 'em
And the Windies called him 'Iron Bottom'.

To be as funny as Groucho Marx
(I'd more chance of being the cat that barks.)
These are things I longed to be
But I was too busy being me.

If you have enjoyed this book,

why not read last year's offering,

I Look At It Like This?

Visit Amazon to buy it, along with more copies of this book.

Turn over to read some of the 100% 5* reviews

100% 5* reviews

- Another brilliant dip-in/dip-out book from Alton Douglas. Lots of anecdotes from his time in show business, including descriptions (mainly positive but not exclusively so) of many well known people that he came across around the clubs and TV studios. Lots of one-liners and funny rhymes to make the sides ache with laughter. Thoroughly recommended.
- As always a fantastic read from a wonderful entertainer.
- I was laughing out loud on the first page. A very funny book full of anecdotes and jokes. An excellent Christmas present.
- In a long and varied career, Alton has appeared in almost every UK theatre of note and worked with just about every star name over the last sixty years! He has a tale to tell about most of them, and nearly all (but not every one!) with fondness and affection.
- He has a relaxed and easy to read style and if you enjoy hearing about life in show business (warts and all!) over the last sixty years, Alton's latest book of 'Anecjokes' is one that you will like!

Printed in Great Britain
by Amazon

31315388R00086